SAGE
LIVING

SAGE LIVING

Decorate for the Life You Want

Anne Sage

Photographs by Emily Johnston

CHRONICLE BOOKS
SAN FRANCISCO

For everyone who has helped to light my path, and for everyone who is forging one of their own.

Library of Congress Cataloging-in-Publication Data available.

ISBN 978-1-4521-4006-3

Manufactured in China

Designed by Allison Weiner

10 9 8 7 6 5 4 3 2

Chronicle Books LLC
680 Second Street
San Francisco, California 94107
www.chroniclebooks.com

Contents

INTRODUC

Our homes are like mirrors. An organized yet lived-in kitchen reflects its owner's passion for cooking and entertaining. A spare, restrained space speaks of inhabitants who value simplicity. A playful, eclectic apartment may hint at a first-time renter exploring personal style through decor. From our passions and interests to the stage of life through which we're passing, our living spaces are extensions of ourselves.

TION

But it works the other way too. Just as our personalities influence our homes, we can shape our environment to help us push through challenges or nurture aspects of our character that we'd like to see flourish. The busy mom who wants to care for herself more may cultivate a weekly habit of arranging flowers on her bedside table. The artist who wants to transition from hobbyist to pro might renovate a spare bedroom into a studio. The symbolism of these acts has as much power as the acts themselves. It signifies our desire for change and becomes a self-fulfilling prophesy in the realization of our dreams.

So instead of decorating for the life you have, why not decorate for the life you want? This book helps you do exactly that by introducing you to a host of inspiring individuals who have authored their own home stories and altered themselves in the process. On a budget? Meet a mom and small business owner who downsized out of necessity but who loves her cozy new bungalow more than her previous sprawling mansion. On a quest for better health? Read about a holistic nutritionist who revamped her kitchen to nourish her budding career as well as her growing family. Transitions like these aren't easy, but they are possible—and hearing about them from real people enables you to visualize your own transformation.

Although the idea for this book materialized slowly over the course of a year, the seed was planted when I moved into my first apartment. Sure, I'd had other apartments, but this was the first time I'd navigated the real estate process by myself, the first time I'd signed a lease with only my name on it, the first time I'd be living without family, a roommate, or a husband. I was thirty years old, and I was terrified. I arrived in Los Angeles from San Francisco having walked away from an ailing marriage and from the business into which I'd poured both my heart and my finances. I brought with me one suitcase, six grocery sacks, and a handwritten list of five goals. At the top of that list was the very journey upon which I had just embarked: live by myself for at least one year. As I carried my bags up the stairs and into the unknown, I felt trepidation but also an overwhelming need to prove that I could in fact survive alone. Because, truth be told, I didn't believe myself the least bit capable of doing so.

Today, my life looks very different than it did then. When fear and self-doubt come knocking, I simply remind myself how far I've come since those first frightening days. This period of living alone has been a time steeped in reflection. Every question about my house (Should I shop vintage or new? How long can I go without a sofa, anyway?) has provided the chance to ask at a more profound level, Do I want this in my life? Do I *need* this in my life? As I've become more intentional about my interior, I've learned what's important to me and what I can let go. I've witnessed firsthand the power of a mindful home to alter my outlook, boost my confidence, and empower me to take my destiny into my own hands.

Through my work as a design and interiors blogger at *The City Sage* and also as a cofounder of the online lifestyle publication *Rue Magazine*, I've become more attuned to the immeasurable ways in which people adapt their decor to further their dreams. This awareness filtered my lens and focused it on the twenty-eight spaces contained here, all of which have been designed to advance their occupants along a course of personal growth. I visited their homes and learned the details of their lives, and I've done my best to tell their stories with the mix of aesthetic reverence and emotional resonance I believe they deserve. I've also highlighted key steps on their paths so you can chart your own course to living well.

Most of all, I've made this a volume you'll want to reach for no matter what your situation. One with images you'll leaf through for decor inspiration before a sunny morning trip to the flea market. But also one with stories you'll linger over when nighttime falls and shadows dim the path ahead. Because I've walked that daunting path, and I believe that whatever your goals, your surroundings can help crystallize who you are, where you've been, and the direction you'd like to head. This book is the road map to a destination in which your home and your heart sing in harmony.

CONNECT

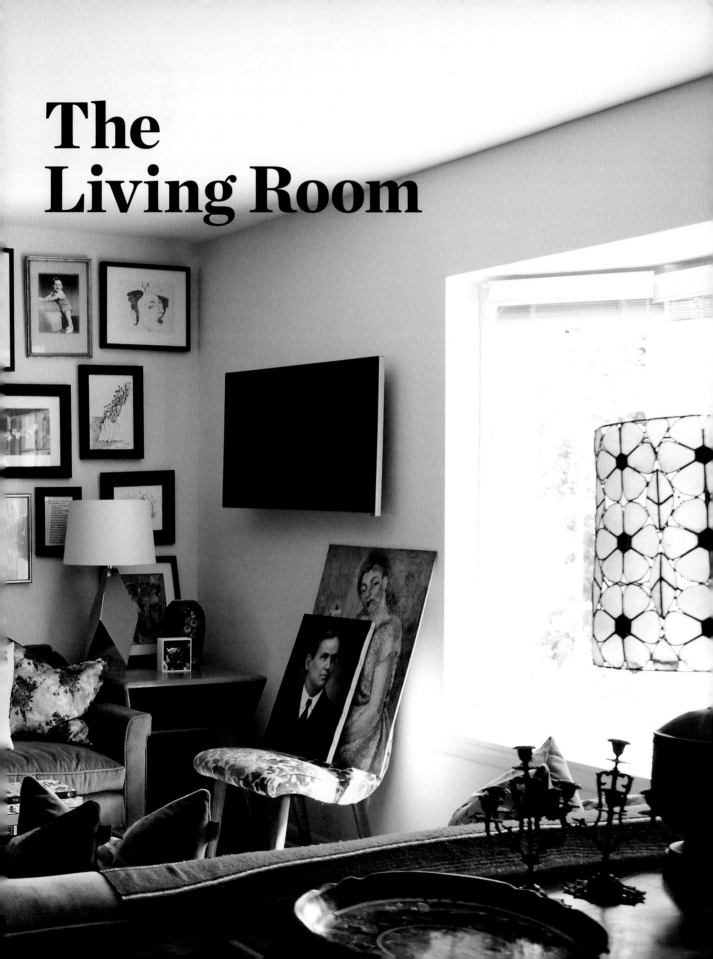

The Living Room

f the kitchen is the heart of the home, then the living room is its soul. Our homes witness the sharing of both our happiest and our hardest times, from tackling the crossword as a family on the sofa every Sunday to gathering with girlfriends to mourn a breakup. Common spaces designed to enrich interpersonal interaction not only elevate our highs, they better enable us to weather the lows. What's more, they help us affirm our own identities through our decor. In the living room, we let down our guard and open up our self.

When we bond over a DVD marathon or proudly display our grandmother's travel memorabilia, we reveal our interests and our history—vital aspects of what makes us tick. An inviting, thoughtful living space not only reinforces our own values, it also encourages everyone who inhabits the space to relax and confide a piece of themselves. This reciprocal sharing in turn furthers an intimacy that Nana didn't anticipate when she willed you her souvenir spoon collection.

Or perhaps she did. After all, the social interactions of our grandparents' generation had a significantly more tangible—and thus more enduring—quality than those we experience today. Letters, phone calls, and face-to-face visits were the rule, not the exception to it. As multitasking fragments our attention and status updates make sound-bite communication the norm, lasting relationships require an increasingly concerted effort to initiate and maintain, and they become all the more necessary because most of us aren't reaping their rewards on a daily basis. Suddenly, that wine-fueled girls' night takes on a significance that belies its frivolity.

Any living room can be modified to cultivate connection. Start by reflecting on your passions and favorite pursuits to shed light on your values. Consider the objects you'd like to incorporate and the activities you'd like to promote, and disregard the ones you don't. Once you've spent some time on this type of introspection, you can more easily identify the decor elements that define you and then take steps to implement them—whether that means instituting a more strategic layout, establishing a more intentional atmosphere, or adding more nostalgic touches.

This chapter features four homeowners who adapted their living areas in response to their desire to engage more profoundly with their loved ones and with themselves. They include a floral artist who traded a mansion for a modest abode when a near-fatal accident left her craving a more vibrant existence; an illustrator who finally separated work from play and discovered a deep well of peace in the process; a photographer and avid traveler who put away her passport but not the curiosity that motivated her wanderlust; and a publicist who flourished in the wake of a breakup by staking claim to the territory beyond her comfort zone. Each space is as unique as the individuals and situations that gave rise to it, yet each illustrates the ability of thoughtful design to foster more meaningful interactions.

Of course, not every decision involved in decorating your living room will arise from a connection-driven mindset. Some choices will depend on pragmatism alone. Still others will stem from an inexplicable yet undeniable instinct for what you'd like to see in the space. But approach decorating your living room as a chance to enhance your relationships, and you'll find that even those seemingly indefinable instincts tap a deeper need that's waiting to be satisfied. Before long you'll have a space that says, "Take a seat. Make yourself comfortable. Let's get acquainted."

Connect with Calm

Drawing New Lines

When one family member works from home, a few space-planning challenges might present themselves. When two do it, a carefully considered layout becomes crucial. Add in a growing toddler and the claustrophobic realities of Manhattan real estate, and some serious sacrifice—as well as serious patience—is necessary. Such was the case for illustrator and lifelong New Yorker Samantha Hahn, who years ago resigned herself to the allowances required of living and working in close quarters.

However, a tipping point arrived when Samantha and her husband, David, decided to give their young son a sibling. The threesome (with a baby on the way) decamped across the East River to Brooklyn, where they now occupy the top floor of an 1890s limestone walk-up. In pleasing contrast to their previous apartment, both husband and wife now have their own respective offices. Samantha doesn't miss her days at a drafting table squeezed beside the sofa. What's more, she now finds herself in possession of something wholly unfamiliar and decidedly delightful: a living room that she can reserve exclusively for, well, living. Which is exactly what she's done.

WILL BARNET
The Pennsylvania Academy of Fine Arts   December 6–January 3, 1974

Room to Breathe

Samantha's first objective was to cultivate calm throughout the space. Because her commute consists of a single step from the adjacent room, she wanted an especially serene vibe to signal the transition from workday to after-hours. She used the opportunity of the move to perform a ruthless edit of her possessions, ultimately arriving in this larger Brooklyn apartment with fewer pieces than she had in her small Manhattan abode. She then emphasized the room's lofty interior with a coat of soft gray paint and a simple globe ceiling pendant. The final touch, the removal of the interior door between the living room and Samantha's studio, fosters an even greater degree of openness. The minimal decor combined with the airy architectural envelope makes the room feel like a deep, slow exhale at the end of a long day.

Quiet Curation

From among the many elements that Samantha culled in the trip across the bridge, the family's art collection experienced the most marked edit. A born artist raised by professional artist parents, Samantha had acquired several decades' worth of prints, paintings, and photos that she'd heretofore displayed en masse. Yet in the interest of creating a more restful atmosphere in the current living room, she's limited herself to only a few large pieces on the wall. A lithograph rests above the fireplace, and a photographic color study hangs over the sofa—both pieces selected for their bold, simple shapes and limited color palettes. The eye travels less and lingers longer than it would had Samantha replicated her previous gallery wall arrangements. The resulting simplicity of this new visual experience reinforces the room's sense of studied ease.

The living room's layout facilitates downtime.

Minimal decor makes the room feel like a deep, slow exhale at the end of a long day.

Rezone and Relax

The living room's layout facilitates downtime, complementing its soothing atmosphere. Absent from the scheme is conversationally oriented seating that takes guests and entertaining into mind. Rather, a few distinct areas encourage pastimes meant for decompressing. A sofa directly faces the television for laid-back viewing, with an adjacent coffee table inviting propped-up feet. This same low table functions as an activity center for Samantha's one-on-one afternoons with her son. And on the far side of the room, a pair of comfortable armchairs and a fully stocked bookshelf supports the trio of avid readers. In this clearly delineated space, Samantha and her family can focus exclusively on what matters most: each other.

Connect with Calm: How to Bring It Home

- Hang only a few large pieces of artwork rather than several smaller ones, using a limited color palette as your guide. If you'd like to incorporate photos, print them all in black and white.

- Devote distinct areas of your space to pastimes that promote relaxation, keeping the items you need for each activity close at hand.

- Identify the aspects of your interior that make you feel at ease and maximize them. For example, if the sunlight through your tall windows brings you peace, leave them unadorned.

Connect
with
Curiosity

Putting Down Roots

To the consummate wanderer, just about the only thing that seems foreign is the idea of staying in one place. After a military upbringing and a subsequent navy career that carried her to locales as far-flung as Sardinia and Tripoli, the last place that Jenifer Altman expected to settle was the landlocked Appalachian town of Asheville, North Carolina. But when she found herself in Brooklyn, overwhelmed by the demands of raising three daughters, she heeded the call of the countryside and hasn't looked back.

For all that the family has gained by settling in Asheville— the stability of routine, the comfort of community, and a spacious 1950s ranch house on a federally designated nature preserve—Jen remains conscious of the tradeoffs inherent to staying in one place. Her own nomadic past fostered in her an insatiable thirst for the exotic and also honed an impeccable eye for color, light, and material that distinguishes her work as a photographer and stylist. Jen wants her daughters to enjoy as broad an existence as possible, even as they reap the benefits of a small-town life. Thus, she's crafted a home that pays homage to the vast horizons beyond her front door.

A muted palette unifies the space.

Jen continually moves, adds, and eliminates pieces in a study of the unexpected.

Adventure on Display

In the living room, where the family gathers most often, Jen has arrayed countless objects on every surface. Her collections range from personal ephemera to natural and historical rarities, and she's assembled them with the same sense of curiosity that served to propel her through her travels. She confines herself to no particular plan, aligns herself with no particular style, and selects items solely according to what intrigues her. Agates and alligator snouts mingle with cacti and cowboy boots. What's more, Jen continually moves, adds, and eliminates pieces in a study of the unexpected. A giant boar's head might face off with a life-sized photo of Athena one day, only to oversee an array of driftwood and deer horns the next. This ever-evolving space embodies the awestruck lens through which Jen encourages her daughters to view the universe.

A Limited Palette

Jen's one point of restraint has been the limited range of hues she's introduced in her decor. Crisp white paint on the walls and fifteen-foot cathedral ceilings create a blank canvas effect to offset the living room's contents. Among Jen's collections themselves, neutrals dominate—selected for their ability to unite the room's disparate elements in a subtly shifting current of faded blacks, weathered whites, and timeworn browns. Yet as much as this muted palette unifies the space, it also emphasizes the details that make each individual piece unique. A shell spirals tighter. A gemstone gleams brighter. Without the distraction of color, objects aren't merely seen, they're examined.

Hands-On Exploration

Given the advanced age and delicate nature of the living room's many treasures, the space could easily read as inaccessible. However, Jen avoids a look-but-don't-touch vibe by incorporating even the most precious items into the family's routine. She's given the girls carte blanche access to the antique credenza that she rescued from a five-hundred-year-old English cottage, and they frequently mine the mahogany drawers for the cache of paper, pastels, and colored pencils within. Similarly, a dozen vintage atlases spend as much time sprawled on the floor for informal geography lessons as they do stacked neatly beside the credenza. And a growing pile of family snapshots remains unframed on the console, begging to be picked up and reminisced over. In her quest to bring the world to their doorstep, Jen has created a living museum that values interaction over observation, imagination in addition to inquiry, and above all a reverence for the wonder of the everyday.

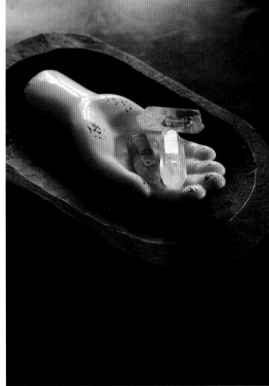

Connect with Curiosity: How to Bring It Home

◆ Incorporate elements informed by your interests into your living space. A love of reading might inspire reproduction prints from first-edition books, while a fascination with the natural world could translate as framed star charts or a tray of semi-precious stones.

◆ Maintain a neutral palette in both furnishings and decor; without the distraction of much color, the details of each object catch the eye more easily.

◆ Encourage interaction with your decor by displaying objects that invite learning and hands-on exploration. Think vintage atlases and globes, nature and photography books, or even a rotating assortment of found black-and-white snapshots.

Connect with Chaos

Downsizing by Design

When most homeowners plan an upgrade, they dream big: larger rooms, higher ceilings, and more amenities. But when Ashley Woodson Bailey relocated from her stately Atlanta mansion to a modest 1950s split-level, small was the order of the day. She traded a fully equipped kitchen for cramped counters and creaky cabinets; polished hardwood floors for weathered planks; a painstakingly landscaped yard for an overgrown patch of forest. And although Ashley and her family now inhabit half their previous square footage, they couldn't be more content.

The move stemmed partly from practical concerns. A head-on auto collision the year before left Ashley unable to accomplish the physical tasks that previously she'd done with ease. Cleaning the sizable suburban house became an impossible undertaking, and chasing her three young children up and down several flights of stairs was out of the question. However, the decision to scale back was as much personal as it was pragmatic. Ashley wanted a home with a compact footprint, one in which she could fully realize her conviction that every day with her family must be embraced to its fullest—an outlook that her near-fatal car accident only served to reinforce.

Ashley designed the living room to be as flexible as possible.

The vibrant aesthetic that characterizes the room echoes the high-energy manner in which the family employs the space.

Fluid Dynamics

For Ashley, the desire to welcome each moment with open, enthusiastic arms results in a constant rush of activity. Because she wanted all day-to-day operations to occur in one central hub, she designed the living room to be as flexible as possible. A wall-mounted TV angles out for early-morning cartoons and breakfast on the couch, then pivots back for a hidden profile when the brood heads off to school. Throughout the day, friends and colleagues frequently take advantage of an open invitation for coffee and collaboration, so occasional chairs dot the perimeter of the room to provide additional seating when needed, and to display framed artwork when not. Finally, Ashley has intentionally left the room's large bay window unadorned in order to foster a front-porch sensibility, and many evenings find her with her husband and a glass of wine as they watch night fall over the neighborhood.

A Working Arrangement

Most notably, Ashley has established her work quarters in the living room as a way to maximize the time she spends around her children. The configuration represents no insignificant sacrifice, since her job as a floral artist requires extensive space. Next to the stairwell, an inexpensive console from a big-box store serves as both work surface and storage for supplies. Its crisp white lines present a facade worthy of a room that receives guests, while its glossy fiberboard finish allows for easy cleanup of the dirt and dings inherent to Ashley's trade. Beneath the cabinet, woven cloth baskets keep toys accessible—and also keep the youngest member of the family at arm's length while his mother works. A vintage flower shop sign demarcates the area where Ashley builds her signature bouquets, its cheerful hues and loopy typeface uniting the work nook with the rest of the room's lively spirit. Functionally as well as visually, the setup manifests Ashley's goal of blending professional and personal into one vivacious whole.

Welcome Wear and Tear

The vibrant, easygoing aesthetic that characterizes the living room echoes the high-energy manner in which the family employs the space. Some decor touches—colorful knickknacks from a mix of styles and eras, an art arrangement that meanders willy-nilly across the wall—embody Ashley's animated approach to life. Others, however, are concessions to the room's nonstop traffic. Where jumping feet and wriggling seats have rendered the sofa threadbare, Ashley has spread a Mexican blanket over the cushions as a quick fix that suffices until the kids are older. Similarly, the wood floors are bare between the sofas so that the coffee table can easily be pushed aside for impromptu talent shows. Rather than resent the scuffs, snags, and stains, Ashley chooses to view them as vital signs that the room is being used exactly as she had hoped.

Connect with Chaos: How to Bring It Home

◆ Accommodate all the day's activities with multifunctional furniture that isn't too precious and can easily be rearranged to suit a number of situations.

◆ If your living space is also your workspace, find ways to delineate between the two for greater appreciation of both—even if the separation is abstract, such as a "no laptops on the couch" rule.

◆ Complement the energy of a high-traffic living room with an eclectic mix of decor pieces that defy the rules of color and pattern in favor of inducing smiles and special memories.

Connect with Character

Moving On and Moving Up

Change has a habit of presenting itself not as a trickle but as a deluge. When it knocked on Laura West's door, it simultaneously delivered a promising job opportunity and signaled the end of a long-term relationship. So Laura did what any newly single, upwardly mobile professional might. She moved to a new city—the geographic equivalent of diving in and letting the river of change propel her forward. Longing to put behind her the history contained in an Atlanta apartment she'd shared with her boyfriend, the Georgia native went in search of a place to call her own, one that gave her a fresh personal start and also encapsulated the exciting possibilities of her new position as social media director for the popular decor retailer Layla Grayce.

Laura found her future by looking to the past. She returned to Athens, Georgia, where she'd attended university and where her brother still lived, and she serendipitously stumbled on a vacancy in a nineteenth-century textile mill that she'd admired from afar during college. The moment Laura walked into the refurbished industrial unit with its soaring ceilings and exposed brick walls, she knew she'd found the ideal blank slate. Her former housing situation had demanded compromise, the give-and-take required of cohabiting with a partner. But now with only herself to please, Laura embarked upon a full-scale investigation into her own identity.

Laura has juxtaposed wildly disparate textures and materials, sizes and shapes.

Go to Extremes

Laura's previous apartment saw her accommodating another's preferences with meet-in-the-middle neutrals and a decidedly absent design voice. With the primary objective of establishing a stronger personality in her new living room, Laura has juxtaposed wildly disparate textures and materials, sizes and shapes. The hypnotic burl of olive wood plays against the magnetic polish of solid brass. Airy Lucite mingles with densely lacquered bamboo, while sumptuous velvet and feathery flokati dance in concert with the loft's raw concrete shell. Oversized black frames float in a field of pure white, enhancing the bold, graphic appeal of the artwork they display. The resulting high-contrast effect, like a volume dial that cycles from mute to full blast, can't help but make itself heard.

Revel in Excess

Laura's greatest indulgence has evolved from a casual interest into a comic obsession. For years, the self-professed animal lover would pick up the occasional cat statue that caught her eye at a thrift store or flea market. Now, with no one to stop her, Laura has allowed feline figurines to overrun the house. A black ceramic panther roars on the coffee table; two red jaguar lamps flank a console; a three-foot porcelain Persian holds court on the floor. The over-the-top collection is both humorous and eye-catching, and a decorative embodiment of Laura's wry, ironic sense of humor. With this immersion in unapologetic kitsch, Laura has learned that skirting the limits of good taste is exactly her style.

Thrill of the Hunt

Although Laura's new job in the interiors industry has given her a greater appreciation for high-end furnishings, one thing it hasn't changed is her determined DIY streak. In fact, armed now with a broader design vocabulary, she more easily articulates the aesthetic she sees in her mind's eye—and ascertains creative ways to achieve it. Laura regularly scours secondhand resources for standout pieces on which she can put her unique stamp. Her patient yet persistent decor stalking has led her to everything from a mint-condition Milo Baughman credenza (purchased for a jaw-dropping seventy-five dollars) to a Parsons chair by the same designer (a mere ten dollars and patiently awaiting new upholstery). Her favorite piece of artwork is actually a sheet of wrapping paper rescued from the discount bin. In fact, nothing in the deceptively luxe living room cost Laura more than one hundred dollars. The more unique the find, the greater the pride she takes in it, for every hour of hunting and refurbishing represents an investment in the limitless potential of her new life.

Connect with Character: How to Bring It Home

- No matter what your style preference, indulge in the opportunity to take your decor to extremes. Go bold with color and finish, shape and scale.

- Collections can reveal a sense of humor as well as a sense of style. Display a roundup of quirky figurines, thrifted paint-by-number canvases, or other smile-inducing kitsch.

- Revel in the thrill of the hunt as well as in the finished product. Fixer-up furniture gives you the chance to put a one-of-a-kind touch on your surroundings.

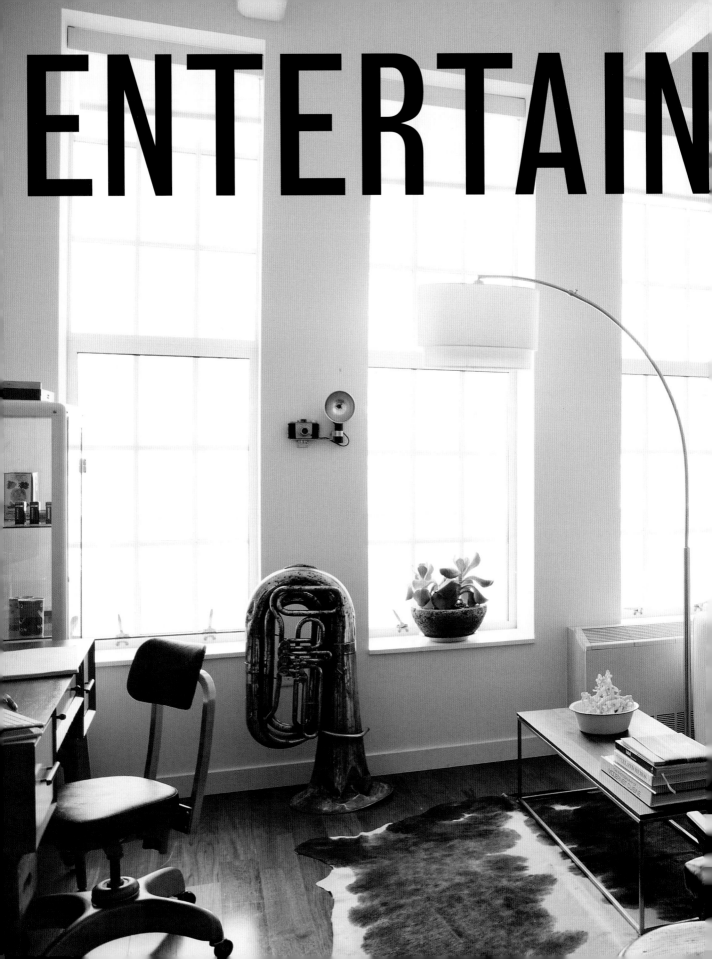

ENTERTAIN

The
Dining Room

The dining table just may be the most well-rounded piece of furniture in the house. It can function as a makeshift desk, junk mail repository, gift-wrapping station, or all three at once! But even in its most versatile moments, the hardworking table may lament that it has missed its true calling: serving up soup-to-nuts meals for a boisterous bevy of friends and family members. Because in reality, many of us would rather picnic in the Antarctic than host a social event *chez nous*.

Indeed, hospitality can be stressful. From wrangling busy guests to shopping for ingredients, from cleaning and cooking to mixing cocktails and monitoring crudités, we get more caught up in the fear of imperfection than in the pleasure of the moment. Halfway through the meal an exhausted hostess finds herself counting the minutes until everyone leaves so she can go to bed. Add the fact that an evening's entertaining easily becomes the next morning's dishwashing deluge, and it comes as no surprise that we've sworn off hosting in favor of takeout and TV dinners.

Yet for all its effort, entertaining offers very real rewards. In the midst of the daily grind, planning a menu or arranging a centerpiece may represent the most creative freedom we experience all week. An afternoon kaffeeklatsch provides the perfect excuse to test that new snickerdoodle recipe on a herd of fellow cookie monsters, rather than eat the entire bowl of dough alone at the kitchen sink. But most importantly, hospitality is a valuable exercise in generosity—an opportunity to open our homes and present our guests with the gifts of our time, attention, and love.

To minimize the output of entertaining and maximize its happy returns, recognize that even the most consummate of hosts makes compromises more often than not. They gather girlfriends for a weekly book club, then trade the trouble of homemade refreshments for a doughnut pit stop on the drive home from the office. Or they invite their thirty nearest and dearest to a lavish holiday dinner complete with letterpress invitations and a signature rum punch, but reserve it as an annual occurrence to heighten guests' anticipation—and to guarantee a 364-day recovery period.

These trade-offs stem from a host's understanding of her own personality (introvert with a fondness for fireside chats, or extrovert who craves a crowd?) and preferences (a pancake brunch for the early bird, an all-hours BBQ for the night owl). Once these inclinations have been defined, the home can then be refined to accommodate them. A fan of the casual daytime drop-in might fill his hutch with mugs and loose-leaf tea, while the amateur mixologist should reserve display space for an ice bucket and bitters. The foodie who prefers front-porch potlucks to full-service feasts may not require a formal dining room at all. Each decor decision gives the host a chance to pour out a measure of herself, while also giving guests the space to sip from the cup of her hospitality.

To get a stronger handle on your entertaining style, think about the gatherings you've hosted—and attended!—that have brought you the most pleasure. Was food the central focus or did it take a backseat to conversation? Do you revel in the preparation of an elaborate affair, or does the spontaneity of a last-minute get-together energize you? What are the elements that make *you* feel welcome when you're a guest, and how can you implement them when it's your turn to host? If you know whether you'd rather cook for six than mix cocktails for twenty, then you'll be better equipped to make decisions about seating and servingware.

Of course, a good party is all about good company, and this chapter has that in spades. We'll visit with a Savannah fashion designer whose elegant, eclectic style gives new meaning to old-fashioned hospitality; a Los Angeles couple whose home serves as a de facto bed and breakfast for their tribe of nomadic friends; a New York City event designer who reconfigured her apartment to throw the elaborate affairs she's staked her career on; and a Brooklyn chef who traveled the world to learn that the warmest welcome lies in the comforts of home. As any of them can attest, anxiety will always arise when the pleasure of guests is on the line—but a strategic blend of forethought and focused design can promise fewer headaches, and more hugs, handshakes, and hellos.

Entertain with Artistry

Shifting Focus

A career change presents no shortage of challenges. When it requires a complete overhaul, it can be downright disorienting. Just ask Brooke Atwood. After years of owning a successful women's boutique, the single mother left her hometown of Oxford, Mississippi, to attend the prestigious Savannah College of Art and Design, in Georgia. Faced with a city of strangers and stretched thin by the demands of school, work, and parenting, Brooke put her head down and soldiered through.

When she lifted it four years later, it was with delight to discover that she had acquired not only a master's degree but also an expansive network of friends and colleagues—as well as a deep reverence for the captivating history and personality of Savannah itself. She simultaneously realized that her single-minded pursuit of her goals had necessarily rendered her somewhat apathetic to her surroundings. Equipped now with the skills and support to achieve her lifelong dream of becoming a fashion designer, Brooke set about creating a space where she could celebrate her new life in old Savannah style.

The dining room's refined irreverence aligns with Brooke's contemporary take on good old Southern hospitality.

A Spirited Salon

Savannah has always been known for its vibrant cultural community, a reputation that Brooke ardently upholds. In the living room, she surrounds guests with objects that spark conversation and creativity. Oversized volumes on photography and illustration line the shelves. A library of *Vogue* magazines includes every issue since 1976. The musically inclined can browse the extensive collection of records that await a spin on Brooke's vintage turntable, and a piano and guitar stand at the ready for spontaneous duets. Step into the dining room, and a gallery wall populated entirely by works from local artists pays homage to Savannah's thriving art and design scene. With her emphasis on entertaining as an active exchange of ideas and inspiration, Brooke continues a vital tradition of the city she now calls home.

Polish with a Twist

Every proper sit-down needs a nexus worthy of the gatherings it hosts. Brooke has installed exactly that in the dining area, furnishing the room with a refined irreverence that aligns with her contemporary take on good old Southern hospitality. A Victorian-era table grounds the space with its weighty construction and burnished mahogany finish. Six tulip chairs flank the stately antique, chosen both for their pedestal shape—which echoes the table's silhouette—and for their space-age whimsy, which offsets its gravitas. Mismatched armchairs at the head and foot of the table give a wink to formality, and on a nearby console are marble bust lamps with metallic silver shades straddling the line between classic and cool. Up to eighteen diners can assemble for Brooke's go-to menu of fast-food chicken and biscuits, assured of an evening at once jovial and genteel.

Untamed Heart

Brooke takes an exuberant party atmosphere as a sign that she's properly doing her job as a hostess. She therefore punctuated her interior with boisterous accents that encourage guests to let their hair down. Vermillion velvet seating spices up the living room, its fiery presence complemented by the touches of tangerine, carnation, and tomato in Brooke's book and art displays. Mirrored metallics—on end tables, on side chairs, and even on lampshades—flash in the moonlight for a sophisticated disco-ball effect. Not content to let just color do the talking, Brooke invoked the animalism of the jungle with a leopard-patterned pillow for the sofa and a zebra-print cowhide for the floor. And in one final stroke of character, a garden flamingo nests among the leaves of a houseplant. His hot hue and offbeat charm join with the rest of the decor to issue Brooke's desired invitation: a resounding call to get a little wild.

Entertain with Artistry: How to Bring It Home

- Provide no-pressure access to cultural pastimes. Instruments—even silly ones like a tambourine or ukulele—bring out hidden talents, while art, travel, and fashion books ignite the imagination.

- Provide a single focal point around which guests can gather for group interaction. A dramatic dining arrangement works

  wonders, but in the absence of a large dining room a coffee table surrounded by plenty of seating will do too!

- Foster spirited conversation with equally energetic decor. Play with contrasting styles, vivid colors, and graphic patterns for a dynamic mix.

Entertain with Altruism

Open Hearts, Open Home

If generosity is the key to hospitality, then Jessica and Jonathan Taylor have a shot at "Hosts of the Century." The couple have structured their entire existence around their commitment to giving back, using it as the framework for both their marriage and their business. The latter traces its origins to the frustration that a fresh-from-college Jessica felt toward the bureaucratic red tape preventing her from truly making a difference in her chosen field of social work. She directed her sights to her longtime hobby—refinishing and selling discarded furniture to raise money for the homeless—and turned it into a career. A flea-market stand became an online shop, which then came to provide event rentals, and today the business, called Taylor + Taylor, offers full-service interior design with an emphasis on elevating the unclaimed.

Jonathan, for his part, stocks his wife's inventory from pit stops at the thrift stores and estate sales he encounters through his work tutoring immigrant students across Southern California. Together they bring their principles of altruism to life in their Burbank bungalow, opening it to everyone from Canadian missionaries to Congolese refugees. With that rotating cast of houseguests in mind, they've edited and arranged their ever-expanding trove of vintage treasures to create an airy, inviting space that always has room for one more.

A mix of ink and charcoal illustrations evokes a Renaissance feel.

Lost and Found

From wandering souls to unwanted stuff, Jessica and Jonathan have no trouble making room for people and objects in need of a home. The difficulty instead lies in harnessing their hunter-gatherer instincts without hampering their motley sensibility. Subtle manipulations of proportion and palette steer the Taylors away from cluttered and into curated territory. Their first table, a hefty oak antique, yielded an elegant but encumbered dining area, so they installed iron hairpin legs beneath a weathered teak slab for a daintier yet equally dramatic presence. Diners can pull up one of six different chairs that are mixed in personality yet matched in midcentury style. Smaller elements follow the same protocol, with weighty ceramics unified by their light, creamy finish and ponderous curios by their flashes of brass. The deliberate play of contrast leads to an aesthetic that is at once eclectic, unfussy, and utterly unique.

Sun Chasers

Jessica and Jonathan rarely awaken to an unoccupied guest room, meaning they're more likely to host breakfast than any other meal of the day. They've therefore effected in the space a bright yet gentle quality of light suited to the rhythms and rituals of morning. To counter the dimness caused by low ceilings and west-facing windows, while still avoiding the harsh glare of incandescent bulbs, the Taylors encourage as much natural illumination as possible. No curtains, blinds, or even screens obscure the windows in the dining room. For the walls, the couple selected an especially reflective shade of white—and chose a satin finish over the more commonly used eggshell to infuse what little sunshine does enter the room with a luminous glow. The resulting serene atmosphere eases everyone into the day.

Studied Display

Jessica and Jonathan view their drop-in sleepover policy as a small contribution to the endeavors of their friends, many of whom earn a scant living furthering nonprofit causes. With this socially conscious cast of characters, talk often turns to politics or philosophy for an intellectual milieu that the couple furthers with their decor. Stacks of books sprout from every surface, sparking discussions as well as lending a hand to prop up a plant, offset an *objet*, or complete a color story. However, the real honor goes to the art arrangement above the sofa. The mix eschews photos or prints in favor of ink and charcoal illustrations, which evoke a Renaissance feel. Elaborate gilt frames suggest a pricelessness to their contents, though the assortment consists mostly of pages rescued from crumbling portfolios and therefore cost less than the average museum admission. From Enlightenment to Bauhaus, the gallery pays indirect homage to the movements that altered the course of history, and reinforces the Taylors' desire to change the world, one guest a time.

Entertain with Altruism: How to Bring It Home

- Honor your love of found objects but prevent a hodgepodge effect by curating your treasures according to a limited range of textures and materials.

- Invite overnight guests into your morning routine by creating a soothing, welcoming atmosphere. Soft hues and a gentle quality of light encourage bonding over coffee and quiet conversation.

- For a gallery wall that appeals to the eye and to the intellect, hang unexpected art such as vintage architecture blueprints, discarded illustration portfolios, or even pages from disintegrating books.

Entertain with Abundance

Continental Influence

Like the stock of an ancient Cabernet cultivar, the roots of Julia Lake's instinct for entertaining go deep. The events expert hails from Napa Valley, where her winemaker father gave her an appreciation for that industry's timeless hospitality traditions. When Julia wasn't soaking up the mellow of the vineyards, she was traveling abroad to Germany, where she reveled in the old-world embrace of her parents' home country. The pleasure of holidays and get-togethers with family near and far planted seeds that grew into the themed parties that Julia frequently threw in high school. The young hostess poured herself into planning and executing every detail of the elaborate affairs, partly for her own expression but mostly for the enjoyment of her friends, who to this day can recall the fun of those now-legendary affairs.

Years later, when her marriage prompted a move to New York City, Julia brought with her the dual perspective that now informs her hallmark entertaining style: the casual spirit of her California upbringing combined with the lavish aesthetic of her European heritage. This outlook not only distinguishes the weddings and celebrations that Julia designs through her firm, Julia Lake Parties, it also informs the decor of the historic Cobble Hill flat she shares with her husband and their dog, Otto von Pickles. Design decisions throughout facilitate Julia's signature gatherings while also accounting for her time and space constraints. For as her business flourishes and her workload increases, Julia more than ever needs her home to serve as both a testing ground for her creativity and a resting ground for her friends.

Set the Threshold

Julia takes pains to greet invitees with a warm welcome and a cold drink. However, the layout of her unit didn't immediately lend itself to gracious receptions. Open the front door and step into a small enclosure that, due to its adjacency to the kitchen, operates most logically as a breakfast nook. Julia initially furnished it as exactly that, but the setup wasn't striking a welcoming note. So she squeezed the table and chairs into the living room, then transformed her erstwhile dining area into a proper entryway. Now, a three-tiered console occupies the space. It showcases the floral arrangements and styled vignettes that Julia rotates for seasonal impact, as well as photos and mementos for a personal feel. Most importantly, a fully-stocked bar holds a place of honor on the top shelf, enabling Julia to enforce her "cocktail in hand within thirty seconds" rule for visitors. Thanks to the new arrangement, and to space sacrificed elsewhere in the apartment, a party at the Lake household begins the moment a guest arrives.

Stand and Deliver

Although Julia loves to host a crowd, she has long since accepted that her small home will never accommodate more than a handful of people for a sit-down meal. She's therefore decorated it for an equally appealing alternative: stand-up occasions that promote shoulder-to-shoulder socializing. In lieu of many chairs, versatile tables of all shapes and sizes populate the space. The array includes an antique captain's desk that frequently serves as a buffet—though in order to discourage hungry guests from congregating around a sole source of sustenance, Julia also distributes smaller servings of food throughout the house. Partygoers mingle about, delighting in discovering appetizers on the étagère, cheese on the china hutch, desserts on the dresser. By forgoing seating for surfaces, Julia both maximizes the capacity of her gatherings and promotes a bustling, dynamic atmosphere.

A party at the Lake household begins the moment a guest arrives.

By forgoing seating for display surfaces, Julia maximizes the capacity of her gathering and promotes a bustling, dynamic atmosphere.

Top-Tier Organization

Like many an avid entertainer, Julia has accumulated an extensive mix-and-match array of barware, china, and other serving essentials. In order to keep each item accessible and guarantee it a spot in her active rotation, Julia stores the entire collection in a glass-doored cabinet and curates each shelf according not to function but to finish. A phalanx of wine bottles grounds the display; crystal stemware and highball glasses scintillate from the second tier; the next layer highlights Julia's prized heirloom porcelain; and for the crowning glory, a sterling punch bowl holds court among a retinue of silver flatware, platters, and pitchers. Grouping like materials gives a sense of order and abundance to the diverse assortment. And whether she's bringing to life her vision for a Kentucky Derby brunch or the annual Christmas bash, Julia always knows exactly where to reach.

Entertain with Abundance: How to Bring It Home

- Set a welcoming tone as soon as guests step through the front door. If your home lacks a formal entryway, carve one out with a console table decorated with personal touches or a bar cart stocked with cocktail supplies.

- Don't let an unconventional interior stop you from hosting altogether! Guests won't miss a dining table as long as the party provides plenty of snacks, sips, and spirited conversation.

- A growing collection of glass- and servingware breathes continual new life into your entertaining style, but it can easily become cluttered and hard to manage. Keep it organized and close at hand by storing it grouped by material as well as by function.

Entertain with Authenticity

International Studies

Sometimes you have to leave home to find home, and there's no guarantee that the search will be brief. Jane Coxwell began her quest at the age of eighteen, when a dream of seeing the world prompted her departure from her native South Africa. Jane's journey took her to culinary school in London, then to the South of France, where she plied her chef's skills in the galleys of the luxury yachts that cruise the Mediterranean. Bigger boats—and bigger opportunities—carried her ever farther afield, and soon Jane had visited more countries than even the most seasoned diplomat. Yet the broader her travels, the greater her realization that people everywhere crave the same simple pleasures of a well-prepared meal and loved ones to share it with.

This observation streamlined Jane's approach to food, resulting in a lack of pretension that caught the eye of a high-profile client based in New York. Persuaded by the job offer of a lifetime but also by the chance to trade her storage unit for a space of her own, Jane signed a lease on a Williamsburg apartment that she's since designed to embody the straightforward ethos that informs her cooking and her life. Now, when she's not sailing the seas, she's home offering all who enter the universal satisfaction of good food and great company.

Staple Ingredients

Jane builds each dish on a basic foundation that she can take in any direction with the addition of different herbs and spices. Applying this trusty formula, she selected her large decor elements to form a blank canvas conducive to her living space being transformed for riotous poker games and relaxed wine tastings alike. Gridded shelving overlooks a sturdy travertine table and molded shell chairs, and a long linen sofa maintains a low profile opposite a midcentury desk and powder-coated cabinets. Broad, supportive seating emphasizes comfort as well as style. The clean-lined, contemporary furnishings anchor but don't overwhelm the space, and a monochromatic white palette unites it all. Like a hearty broth that acts as a versatile foundation for Italian basil, Thai mint, or Turkish dill, Jane's furnishings abet energies and activities of all kinds.

Garnish to Taste

Jane most loves travel for the ability of foreign sites, sounds, and smells to enhance the present moment. Just as she seeks to replicate the same sense of heightened attention with the food she prepares, Jane wanted to craft an environment that encourages her guests to focus on the immediacy of their surroundings and on each other. She therefore employed a careful application of color to develop a layer of visual interest that intrigues the eye without overly distracting the viewer. A variety of saturated yet subtle hues materialize through sources such as the oversized map above the sofa, the globe on the bookshelf, and an assembly of colorful soda bottles throughout. No single shade dominates, and a balance between warm and cool prevails. The mix feels organic and uncontrived, and it yields a dynamic hum of energy that attunes visitors more closely to the happenings at hand.

Clean-lined, contemporary furnishings anchor but don't overwhelm the space, and a monochromatic white palette unites it all.

Souvenir Style

Each new destination that Jane explores only increases her longing to make the earth seem a little smaller through communal experiences of food and culture. She returns home with an eagerness to impart her infectious passion—and a jam-packed suitcase to help her do exactly that. Her souvenirs blanket the apartment, sparking stories and revealing aspects of global life both wondrous and mundane. A coffee sack from New Zealand testifies to the far-ranging appeal of a steaming cup over conversation. A massive whale vertebrae honors the collaborative endurance of the only remaining Caribbean tribe permitted to land their catch through traditional methods. Food tins from diverse locales speak to the ubiquities of daily life, no matter how exotic their origins. Each travel token represents a tale of shared humanity as well as Jane's desire to weave common threads the planet over. For if she can't bring her loved ones around the world, she'll bring the world to them!

Entertain with Authenticity: How to Bring It Home

- An unfussy interior lets company and conversation take center stage. Keep furniture mostly neutral with a focus on comfort for a relaxed and inviting atmosphere.

- When adding color to a laid-back space, incorporate it through objects that serve more than just a decor function—books, photos, and engaging artwork add color organically to maintain an unstyled sensibility.

- Displayed travel souvenirs impart an infectious sense of curiosity, leading to stories and sharing among guests. No need for an exotic vacation; intriguing pieces can come from across the world or simply across town!

NOURISH

The
Kitchen

To watch a child eat is to witness one of life's most pure and primal pleasures. His single-minded intent as he devours a wedge of watermelon from tip to rind, juices running down his chin and joy filling his eyes. Her noisy, impatient gulps as she drinks from the hose on a hot summer's day, seeking only to quench her thirst so she can return to the serious business of play. Kids eat when they're hungry, stop when they're full, and don't spare a second thought for food unless it's on a table in front of them. A toddler views food as a simple tableau of sense and satisfaction.

Then, somewhere along the way from preschool to prom, the scene becomes complicated. We realize that a hot fudge sundae remedies all manner of ailments. We discover that some families don't buy cheese because it upsets their digestion, some because it comes from a cow, and some because it goes straight to Mom's hips. That bite of pasta is no longer just a forkful of noodles and sauce; it's a heaping helping of physical, emotional, relational, even religious and political implications.

The complexity of our edible landscape is understandable, even expected. From juice fasts to celebratory feasts, food plays an important role in the expression of our personal values and our cultural identities. However, the maze of information and influences surrounding food does turn something capable of bringing us much pleasure and good health into an overwhelming source of anxiety and uncertainty—which in turn obscures our instincts no matter what our mealtime motivations. Whether we want to eat more whole grains or consume less sugar, slim down a size or beef up our school-lunch repertoire, we need a place where we can quiet the noise and make our own individual choices about what lands on our plates.

That place, of course, is the kitchen. The right layout can encourage order and flow to make slicing and dicing a breeze. The right tools take that must-try muffin recipe off your favorite baking blog and put it in your hands. And the right decor accents remind you that as much as food energizes our bodies and delights our taste buds, every morsel can also be a show of love for our families, our planet, and ourselves.

A successful kitchen starts with a cook who understands her own culinary style, so spend some time identifying yours. Do you prefer to cook alone as a meditative exercise or would you rather lead a team of volunteer sous-chefs? Do you pore for hours over cookbooks to plan a dinner menu, or would you prefer to improvise with whatever is on hand? Perhaps you're content with a low-effort weeknight meal routine, but you could spend the entirety of each weekend baking breads and pastries to share with the office on Monday morning. A firm grasp on your kitchen habits and inclinations helps you prioritize your storage space, invest in the tools you'll use most, and surround yourself with the decor elements that make the space more than simply one in which to prepare food.

Of course, when it comes to kitchen design, the variety of "right" answers rivals the seemingly infinite assortment of yogurt flavors in the dairy aisle. This chapter serves up the stories of a resourceful San Francisco couple who embarked on an eco-friendly kitchen remodel to reinforce their ethos of living simply and sustainably; an artist and activist who stirs a message of kindness and hope into each meal she prepares on her Los Angeles stove top; a food stylist whose Atlanta cupboards, counters, and cooking all pay homage to her rich heritage; and a Copenhagen nutritionist whose commitment to holistic wellness helped her start anew in a foreign country—and find a career in the process. Through trial and error, these creative cooks have determined the custom mix of ingredients for kitchens that feed the soul.

Nourish with Humility

Scaling Back

Audrey Bodisco and Karl Aguilar never expected to become homeowners, let alone design and renovation experts. Together since college, the pair happily spent the better part of two decades in unassuming rentals that let them lead the double life of their dreams: by day running a neighborhood hardware store, by night funneling their savings toward rock-climbing trips that took them to the farthest reaches—and highest peaks—of the earth. Then, one day they received the news that Audrey had inherited her grandmother's 1927 Craftsman in San Francisco's Sunset District. Soon after, a back injury put a permanent cramp in Audrey's athletic pursuits. Fifteen years of epic expeditions drew to a close as Audrey and Karl traded their climbing harnesses for house keys.

The couple arrived in their new abode to discover an outdated kitchen worsened by serious disrepair. Although Audrey and Karl had worked around contractors and designers for years at their store, they had no real construction or interiors experience to speak of. Yet they eagerly rolled up their sleeves for a remodel that sustained their long-held affinity for modest living. With a little ingenuity and a lot of elbow grease, the two now have a sturdy foothold from which to embark upon the adventure of the everyday.

The open, elemental space underscores the beauty in simplicity.

A mindful renovation embodies a small-footprint philosophy and also dovetails neatly with the home's old bones.

Easy on the Eye

Audrey and Karl began the renovation with a desire to elevate their aesthetic but still uphold the utilitarian ethos that has always served them so well. The principle of "less is more" therefore ruled their every decision. A notable lack of built-in fixtures fosters an effortless vibe. For example, in lieu of a backsplash behind the entire length of counter, Audrey took the path of least resistance and affixed tile only behind the sink. The couple also eschewed upper cabinets, electing to install only two steel shelves above the stove and to cull their kitchen tools to fit the limited storage. And because the majority of their implements live in plain view, Audrey and Karl limited their selection to the most elemental essentials: a squatty stack of hand-thrown pottery, a tidy row of paper-thin glassware, a wall-mounted grid of knives ordered by size. The open, elemental space exudes a pragmatic elegance that underscores the beauty in simplicity.

Seamless Integration

In addition to implementing design that makes an understated visual impression, Audrey and Karl strove for a neutral impact on the house itself. To that end, they focused less on a total face-lift and more on paring down and adjusting what remained to suit their taste. Wood-grain surfaces offer a uniform sensibility with work surfaces, chairs, and table stained exactly to match the preexisting oak floors throughout the house. The sink backsplash employs subway tile to complement the home's pragmatic Craftsman style but features it in a gridded rather than offset pattern for a more contemporary appeal. And the inoperable refrigerator, a relic from a time when appliances occupied less space than today, left in its wake a nook where no modern unit could squeeze. However, shelving transformed the awkward, unusable space into a compact storage area for everything from dried goods to cookbooks. The mindful renovation not only embodies Audrey and Karl's small-footprint philosophy, it also ensures that the new kitchen dovetails neatly with the home's old bones.

Saving Green

Having traveled and climbed in some of the world's most delicate ecosystems, Karl and Audrey hold themselves to a high degree of environmental responsibility. To bring those standards home, they straddled the line between sustainability and affordability to arrive at design decisions that satisfied both their values and their budget. Most notably, rather than dispose of all existing cabinetry, the couple repositioned one row of cupboards that Audrey subsequently refinished and painted. Recessed LED lighting, though costlier upon installation, has since slashed the couple's electricity bills. Finally, the kitchen's limited cupboard space, as well as a large EnergyStar refrigerator, emphasizes fresh over processed food; with no prepared foods to fall back on, Audrey and Karl have watched their percentage of wasted perishables drop to zero. The couple's new kitchen considers their wallet and the planet alike to ensure a more secure future all around.

Nourish with Hope

Drawing from Experience

Art and activism often join forces, but rarely does their alliance yield an outcome as deliciously life-affirming as what comes from the hands of Ruby Roth. A talented painter and illustrator since childhood, and an ardent vegan for nearly as long, Ruby has combined her two lifelong passions into a thriving career. Her quest began in 2003 when, as an art teacher at an elementary school, Ruby wrote and illustrated a picture book to help her students understand the principles behind her dietary choices. The title received massive attention and acclaim, two subsequent releases followed suit, and all three have since been translated into multiple languages. Ruby's books, together with her weekly newsletter and innumerable speaking and press engagements, reach across the boundaries of age, politics, and nationality to deliver a frank yet gentle message of health and social responsibility.

Today, Ruby initiates much of her routine from the kitchen of her home in Los Angeles's Echo Park neighborhood. Ruby shares the 1930s Spanish bungalow with her longtime partner, Justin Bua, and her nine-year-old stepdaughter, Akira, and here she alternates between testing recipes for her upcoming children's cookbook, capturing and communicating her vision of a more peaceful planet, and preparing meals that embody her family's commitment to cruelty-free living. The constant hum of activity begets a bright, busy kitchen where cuisine and conscience meet, and where kindness and diversity are always on the menu.

Sunny Outlook

To deliver her message of positive change, Ruby populates her books with of herds of cheerful animals and bushels of juicy fruits and veggies. She wanted the room where she spends so much of her time to reinforce the same positive energy. To set a vibrant scene, Ruby took advantage of the kitchen's original glass-fronted cabinets to display her colorful library of cookbooks. A selection of multihued ceramic dishes, as well as process sketches from Ruby's archives, round out the mix. Most importantly, though, plants nestle in every nook and cranny. The indoor garden includes rosemary and oregano for cooking, aloe for soothing skin, and ferns and ficus for providing greenery. Ruby's lively, inviting space overflows with the same vibrant optimism as the work she produces there.

Accent on Accessible

Ruby has taken it upon herself to espouse the message that people- and planet-friendly choices needn't require significant time and money. To enhance the efficiency and economy without detracting from its aesthetic appeal, Ruby has adopted the mantra of "recycle and repurpose." She avoids the reported hazard of plastics in the kitchen—as well as the cost of glass containers—by removing the labels from spent nut butter and marinara jars. This never-ending supply of eco-friendly storage then goes on to lend a clean, uniform appearance to the various functional zones into which Ruby has partitioned the countertops. By clustering powdered supplements near the Vitamix and sprouting grasses beside the juicer, and by displaying dried goods across from the range, Ruby keeps flavor and nutrition within easy reach. Final touches, from a spice display in a cement planter to a collection of empty but still eye-catching tea boxes, give objects life beyond their intended purpose. For Ruby, finding a healthful, harmonious flow lies in seeing old standbys with a new eye.

Rather than paint a pristine portrait, Ruby's kitchen depicts modern family life in all its blurry but beautiful watercolor glory.

Flavor Blend

If change indeed begins at home, then Ruby's kitchen is the model of imminent global harmony. When she arrived here in the wake of Justin's divorce, she resisted the urge to revamp the space and chose instead to honor her new family's makeup through a variety of ethnic handiworks. Asian-style pottery and ceramics fill the cupboards, all of it thrown and fired by Akira's Japanese mother. The oversized bamboo bowl of macadamia nuts, an homage to Ruby's Hawaiian upbringing, awaits the call of a tropical snack attack. Finally, colorful embroidered wall hangings pay respect to the historical Mexican influence that radiates just beyond the front door. The somewhat motley assortment is all the more endearing for its discord. For rather than paint a pristine portrait, Ruby's kitchen depicts modern family life in all its blurry but beautiful watercolor glory.

Nourish with Hope: How to Bring It Home

- Bring personality into the kitchen by incorporating decor elements you might not expect in the space. Nestle framed artwork among pantry shelves and hang houseplants above the sink or even from the undersides of cupboards.

- Get a clean, streamlined look while still respecting your budget and the earth. Reuse spent food jars for storing leftovers, bulk spices, and dry goods, creating uniformity by keeping only those with similar features, such as gold lids or slim, cylindrical silhouettes.

- Add a global touch with elements like woven wall hangings and baskets and handmade bowls and planters. Find inspiration everywhere—from a favorite ethnic market to your own family's geography.

Nourish
with
History

Savoring the Past

When it comes to food, childhood suppertime memories can inform adult preferences. For Annette Joseph, a seat at her grandmother's table didn't just give her a taste for home cooking; it shaped her appetite for hostessing, her belief that a thoughtful meal is an expression of love, and ultimately even her career. A first-generation American born to parents of Hungarian origin, Annette recalls spending summers in Budapest, where Sunday lunch was an all-day affair with every aunt, uncle, and cousin contributing to the feast. Cooked over an open fire and consumed under the trees with a pace dictated only by the slow progress of the sun across the sky, the communal repasts impressed on young Annette the convivial spirit that now colors her work as a lifestyle editor and entertaining expert.

Annette knew she wanted to replicate for her own family and friends the same rich associations with food that she enjoyed growing up. The opportunity to build her Atlanta home from the ground up allowed her to implement exacting layout and decor elements for meals that satisfy both the stomach and the soul. Happily, most of the choices Annette made from emotional impulse met a functional need as well—a testament indeed to the wisdom of tradition.

Annette has fused the acts of cooking, eating, and socializing into one seamless flow of warmth.

Open-Door Policy

Like her forebears, Annette approaches cooking as a communal activity. She's at her best when she's simultaneously manning the stove, directing a small army of sous-chefs, and catching up on the latest happenings. She has therefore set up the kitchen to be as intuitive as possible, not only for herself but also for all whom she drafts into service. Stemware hangs directly beneath the wine rack so that anyone can easily play sommelier. Stainless steel lazy Susans in the fridge keep ingredients accessible. Clearly delineated work stations—a cutting board and garbage receptacle next to the washbasin, and cookware storage and utensil crocks near the range—not only prevent collisions when the prep comes to a head, they also let the crew focus more on chatting and less on shuttling from sink to stove. Finally, Annette has culled her tools to the bare essentials of a well-sharpened knife set, a handful of top-quality pots and pans, and zero single-purpose gadgets. After all, one less gimmicky appliance consuming countertop real estate is room for one more volunteer to elbow in and join the fun.

Gather 'Round

The most striking component of Annette's kitchen is the substantial farmhouse table situated in its center. At over six feet long, it seats a hungry hoard, but its narrower-than-usual width guarantees smooth traffic in the space around it. Inset drawers store cutlery and napkins to make it easy for the kids to set the table and feel a part of the action. Of course, the reclaimed oak beauty isn't reserved only for dining; it's also witnessed many a homework, craft, or catch-up session while dinners roasted in the oven. By positioning the versatile and welcoming surface mere feet from where her thoughtful yet exuberant meals emerge, Annette has fused the acts of cooking, eating, and socializing into one seamless flow of warmth.

Go Alfresco

Annette recalls fondly the degree to which a plein air setting enhanced the laid-back atmosphere of her childhood repasts. She therefore incorporated nature-inspired components into her kitchen for a similarly informal feel. Most notably, a fully functioning garage door abuts the room and opens to eliminate altogether the boundary between outdoors and in. Still other touches are more subtle. Accents of leafy green appear throughout. A towering arched window over the main workspace has been left bare in order to usher in natural light and provide an unobstructed view of the patio. And when it comes to surfaces, Annette has selected earthy textures: exposed wood grain for the wide-plank floors, chunky terra-cotta for the dinnerware, and aged metal for the chairs, shelf brackets, and pendant lamps. The result is a space in which, just like those long-ago family gatherings, time slows down and every moment lasts a lifetime.

Nourish with History: How to Bring It Home

- An open-door policy transforms kitchen time into social time. Encourage everyone to lend a hand with clearly established work stations and a streamlined set of quality, easy-to-use tools.

- Foster a convivial atmosphere in the kitchen by creating space for kids and guests during food preparation. A kitchen table provides ample room for homework or hanging out, but even a barstool at the counter will do in a pinch.

- Incorporate reminders of pleasurable meals past into your kitchen decor. Invoke memories of picnic feasts with natural touches, or recall bountiful family-style dinners with a collection of heirloom serving platters.

Nourish with Harmony

Continental Reboot

Love has a way of prevailing against all obstacles. When a vacation romance left Sarah Britton head over heels for a tall, handsome Dane, she emigrated from Canada to Copenhagen to marry him. And when she discovered that her newly adopted country didn't recognize her certification as a holistic nutritionist, she combined her passion for food with her undergraduate fine arts degree and started the blog *My New Roots*. As skillful with a camera as she is with a chef's knife, Sarah quickly acquired a large international fan base as well as acclaim from culinary and wellness institutions alike. To meet demand for her wholesome yet visually arresting approach to seasonal fare, Sarah soon expanded her offerings to include workshops, retreats, and most recently a cookbook—all of which she produced from the cramped kitchen in her studio apartment.

The scale of Sarah's operation finally outgrew her space when she and her husband, Mikkel, welcomed a son, prompting them to purchase an early 1900s flat near Copenhagen's city center. One quick look at the existing kitchen, with its drop ceiling and linoleum floors, and they knew that only a complete overhaul would give Sarah the room she needed to nurture both her growing business and her growing family. A similarly brief glance at their budget told them that in order to fulfill their vision of a kitchen as inspiring as it is functional, they'd have to do the renovation themselves. One year and countless compromises later, the couple has a space that brings to life Sarah's philosophy that a balanced diet is one part knowledge, one part feeling, and one hundred percent vitality.

Theme and Variations

Sarah enters the kitchen armed not with a set of hard-and-fast rules but rather with an appreciation for the therapeutic powers of foods in their natural states. Because she begins each dish with only a few unprocessed ingredients, then follows her instinct for flavor, color, and satisfaction, she needed a layout and equipment that set the tone for graceful improvisation. Deep drawers beneath the counter house dry goods in clear-lidded jars for grab-and-go convenience. Sarah bypassed a hood over the stove in favor of more storage space for her extensive spice collection, which she uses to enliven the large batches of beans and grains that she soaks ahead of time. And in what would be an easy upgrade for any kitchen, a commercial pressure sprayer takes the place of a standard faucet to make cleaning a breeze. Whether she's developing an original recipe for her readers or preparing a pot of lentils for the week, her simple but strategic setup helps Sarah compose meals that sing.

Built-In Benefits

Sarah's favorite element of the kitchen is the banquette installed in the corner. Not only does the snug dining area maximize a tight floor plan, its demeanor also perfectly reflects Sarah's form-meets-function perspective on food. A swing-arm sconce and wall-mounted shelf of cookbooks frame the space while also rendering the nook an extension of Sarah's workspace; many a long winter evening catches her there brainstorming menus in a circle of lamplight. A bench pad in cheerful blue-and-white gingham provides an extra layer of cushioning—plus has the same energizing effect on the eye as a garnish of parsley has on the tongue. Like the sautés, salads, and smoothies that Sarah serves up, the setting feels comforting and invigorating all at once.

The kitchen owes its clean, warm aesthetic to the patience and open-mindedness demanded of a yearlong renovation.

A Generous Pinch of Time

The kitchen owes its clean, warm aesthetic to components not available for purchase: the patience and open-mindedness demanded of a yearlong renovation. Some details resulted from the couple's careful negotiation of each other's tastes, while still others fell to the irrefutable constraints of reality. A subway tile backsplash and raw wood cookbook shelf speak to Sarah's vintage-industrial sensibility; utilitarian prefab cabinetry satisfies Mikkel's affinity for modern lines and finishes. The near impossibility of carrying several hundred pounds of cement up four flights of stairs required Sarah to forgo her dream of concrete countertops in favor of more manageable birch. And when an exhaustive search for hardware yielded nothing the two could agree on, Sarah tapped her ingenuity and fashioned drawer pulls from strips of leather. Just as a long, slow simmer melds disparate ingredients into a product greater than the sum of its parts, the lengthy construction process yielded a unique cohesion that neither Sarah nor Mikkel could have envisioned at the outset.

Nourish with Harmony: How to Bring It Home

- Make mealtime improvisation second nature with a setup that keeps tools and ingredients well-organized and that takes the pain out of cleanup. Even renters can mount storage racks and hooks inside cupboard doors, or swap an average faucet for an industrial-powered one.

- The kitchen can be a place of retreat as well as one of activity. Carve out a corner with seating, atmospheric lighting, and access to cookbooks and notepads for meal planning.

- The kitchen, like any room in your home, won't come together overnight. Focus on achieving a level of basic function to suit your needs, but maintain an open mind that allows elements like dinnerware, hardware, and small decor to evolve over time.

CREATE

The
Home Office

We're all creative, whether we think so or not. From the teacher designing a lesson plan to the marketer delivering a sales pitch, creativity isn't just the domain of the painters, writers, and photographers of the world—and it's not just a hallmark of the professional arena. We put our creativity to use when we assemble an exciting new outfit from the tired old standbys in our closets, or when we massage the household budget so we can afford those Pilates classes. Add the strategic thinking required to navigate the waters of human relationships—a thank-you text to last night's date requires at *least* as many drafts as a college honors thesis—and each day becomes a tapestry of experience woven from threads of ingenuity.

Given the extensive role that creativity plays in every area of our lives, we can heighten and hone it to make our workdays more fluid and our weekends more fun. Like athletes who train for competition, we increase the strength and endurance of our creativity each time we flex it. Every chord on a guitar or collage in a scrapbook strengthens the mental muscles that help us solve problems with efficiency and ease. Moreover, short daily workouts have a greater impact on overall growth than biweekly burnouts. So, just as a bodybuilder hits the gym daily with near-religious fervor, the best way to encourage the consistency so key to creative growth is to reserve a space for its rituals and routines.

When establishing a space for creativity, first consider the building blocks of your particular pastime. A pianist prepares his fingers for a concerto with a steady practice of scales and arpeggios, and a prima ballerina cannot dance a pas de deux without first taking her feet through their paces at the barre. Similarly, the elements of design can serve as the foundation for the creative habit. Select seating that supplies comfort and support for long hours lost in the flow. Any surface can be a canvas for creativity, so prepare walls and floors as well as desks and tables. Install task-appropriate lighting, be it bright for visibility or soft for a mind-wandering mood. And remember that a creative space needn't be spotless for success, yet a system of organization (even if only you understand it!) helps keep supplies at hand. The shape of the net matters less than the fact that it hovers always at the ready to capture inspiration when it arises.

Once you've furnished the groundwork for the space, layer decor as the pianist or the ballerina layers expression for a unique and memorable statement. Emotion feeds the creative impulse, so focus on how the space makes you feel: energized for a morning gathering imagery online, reflective for a meditative afternoon of knitting, focused for the exacting detail of calligraphy. Tokens of others who inspire you, as well as your own past work, can remind you of where you've come from and where you'd like to go on your creative journey. And above all, leave room for the exploration and evolution of projects and ideas. Whether you're escaping into the leisurely folds of dressmaking or building a business from your knack for graphic design, the ideal creative space is one that provides a safe corridor for new endeavors—and a soft cushion for when they fall flat.

Whether your creative space is your home office or simply a corner of your living room, you can augment it to enhance your output and enjoyment—though of course the catalysts for a smooth creative flow are different for everyone. Are you easily distracted by clutter or does a lot of visual stimulation get your juices flowing? Are you at your most productive when sitting, standing, or lounging? Are your genius hours first thing in the morning or late at night? What are the parameters of your creative pursuits, the essential tools, and the physical requirements of your space and of your body? Identify what you need to maximize function, ease, and organization, then bring it to life with everything from seating, lighting, and work surfaces to color, texture, and decor.

The innovators in this chapter have enacted their own shares of creative trial and error. Peek behind the curtains of a Minneapolis couple who launched a branding agency from an industrial loft that

channels the same yin and yang energy that ignites their relationship; a jewelry artisan who solders silver and gold—and straddles the line between craft and commerce—in her Portland attic; an accomplished interior designer whose Austin bungalow hums with the can-do spirit of the DIY movement; and a songwriter turned social media maven who manifested a consulting career from the corner of her San Francisco studio apartment. All have retrofit their spaces for maximum productivity and play, and in so doing have created havens of creative satisfaction.

Create with Contrast

A Magnetic Match

As office mates turned soul mates, Josef Harris and Liz Gardner can attest that opposites really do attract. The two clicked as collaborators at a local Minneapolis periodical, with his thoughtful, thorough approach to content and her exacting eye for design leading them through many a tight deadline. They remained inseparable even after the publication folded, and the only people taken by surprise when their friendship blossomed into romance were Liz and Josef themselves. Nor did it come as a shock to anyone when together they launched a full-service branding firm in their spare time. After all, Josef's playful and reflective view of the world dovetails with Liz's driven, dynamic personality to make them perfect partners in any arena.

At first the pair merged their belongings in the small studio apartment that Josef had occupied for years. Yet after months of growing their joint venture while also maintaining their demanding day jobs—she as the design director for *Mpls.St.Paul Magazine*, he as an accounts manager at an ad agency—Liz and Josef longed for a home that could accommodate their active lives as well as their expanding ambitions. When a refurbished nineteenth-century factory building opened its doors to renters, the couple braved a Minnesota blizzard and moved in immediately. The open, airy loft now serves as a launchpad for Liz and Josef's many endeavors, and as a reflection of the contrasting yet complementary strengths that fuel their relationship.

The space radiates the energy of a continual work in progress.

The design of the airy loft reflects the contrasting yet complementary strengths that fuel Liz and Josef's relationship.

Impermanent Markers

Liz and Josef need their space to be as fluid and flexible as possible. The versatility not only allows their home to moonlight as a conference room or photo set with a few quick adjustments, it also echoes the couple's experimental approach to creative problem solving and allows them to try new layouts with impunity. Large pieces of furniture, from the desk to the kitchen island, have wheels and can easily be pushed aside for a team brainstorm on the floor. The chaise component of the sofa switches seamlessly from the right to the left of the bench seat to suit any situation. Finally, no art hangs affixed to the walls; instead, numerous prints, posters, and drawings in uniform black gallery frames lean in clusters around the room, ready to be rearranged on a whim. Because Liz and Josef know that inspiration can strike at a moment's notice, they've designed their home to be ready when it does.

A Positive Charge

Whether they're designing the visual identity of an independent fashion brand or developing interiors for a new restaurant client, Liz and Josef view each project as a creative wellspring waiting to be tapped. They therefore sought to fill their apartment with the same sense of unharnessed potential that excites them about their work. The industrial nature of the unit, with its exposed ductwork and concrete floors, lays an unfinished foundation for raw elements such as striated marble, exposed wood grain, and galvanized steel pipe. Throw pillows in graphic textiles line the sofa, their high-contrast prints setting off visual explosions along its length. Finally, black-and-white ink drawings dominate the artwork that populates the apartment for an atmosphere more conceptual than complete. The couple's space radiates with all the energy of a continual work in progress.

He Said, She Said

Because their respective character traits contribute equally to the success of both their business and their relationship, Liz and Josef wanted to depict the same give-and-take in their interior. Dogged and determined, Liz favors modern yet timeless pieces that work as hard as she does: a classic tulip table and chairs and a box-cushion sofa that satisfy with their strong, stable presence. Josef, on the other hand, takes a laid-back approach that applies irreverent and unexpected touches, such as the mint-green doors on the media console and the DIY neon tape art that accents the walls. Liz's bold and iconic choices counter the lighthearted nods to Josef's easygoing spirit to create a cohesive whole as striking and memorable as the couple themselves.

Create with Contrast: How to Bring It Home

- Whether you're accommodating multiple occupants, multiple activities, or both, look for multipurpose furnishings that won't hamper the flow of creativity. For example, a counter-height table on casters offers considerably more versatility than a traditional desk.

- Use high-contrast decor to create a stimulating, energetic atmosphere conducive to play and the exploration of new ideas. Graphic patterns or a bold palette will keep the eye and the mind engaged.

- Indulge the tastes of everyone who uses the room—or simply honor different aspects of your personality—by blending a mix of styles and influences into your creative space. Elements both serious and silly can provide limitless inspiration.

Create with Coherence

Balancing Act

The artistic impulse forges a winding and unpredictable path. When she finished college with a degree in jewelry and textiles, Hannah Ferrara assumed she'd have to split the rest of her life between a job that fed her bank account and an off-hours studio practice that fed her soul. And indeed, she spent a number of years postgraduation as an art teacher and gallery manager while continuing her formal, conceptual explorations on the side. Before long, however, the strikingly sculptural yet eminently wearable quality of Hannah's designs caught the eyes of friends and local retailers who encouraged her to sell them, which she now does under the name Another Feather. The company flourished overnight, and five years later, Hannah can barely keep up with demand for the rings, bracelets, and necklaces that she still produces exclusively by hand.

Though she's happily embraced the all-too-rare blessing of making a sustainable living with her craft, Hannah still feels a push and pull between the practical aspects of business ownership and the pure act of creation. A recent move from Asheville, North Carolina, to Portland, Oregon, allowed Hannah and her husband, Malcolm (himself a respected leather artisan), to fashion a space conducive to all facets of their trades. The two now share a light-filled studio on the top floor of their nineteenth-century home and devote each day to nurturing their entrepreneurial and artistic instincts alike.

Order of Operations

Long before a ring or necklace reaches her collection, Hannah has run it through the gauntlet of concepting, development, and testing. Every stage consists of multiple steps, with each as integral as the last to a finished product that fulfills Hannah's vision as well as the needs of her customers. To stratify and streamline her process, Hannah has established a clearly delineated station for each phase. A new piece begins its trajectory as a sketch pinned to a bulletin board, where it percolates while Hannah addresses mundane tasks like email at the desk below. The design then comes to life at various workbenches around the room: one for general assembly, one for detail work, and one for finishing. The completed piece then departs for its new home from the large central table at which Hannah handles all the packaging and shipping. With its task-oriented layout, Hannah's studio honors the creative journey as fully as it does the destination.

Focused Intent

Whether she's fulfilling orders or developing a new product, Hannah prefers an environment free from the distractions of clutter. Although the extensive surface area and vast quantity of tools required of jewelry design make a truly blank slate impossible, Hannah has cleared space wherever she can. In the studio itself she keeps only the implements she reaches for on a daily basis. Hammers, pliers, and files march neatly along one table; fittings occupy a cluster of ceramic dishes on another; and everything else inhabits a credenza in a nearby hallway. Whitewashed walls and floorboards lay a clean foundation, while airy furnishings including a floating desk, slender lamps, and spindly stools leave plenty of room to breathe. The room's bare sensibility helps Hannah's meticulous work—and fresh ideas—flow freely.

Just as Hannah uses a prescribed set of boundaries to structure her creativity, she has shaped the studio around the few natural materials essential to her routine.

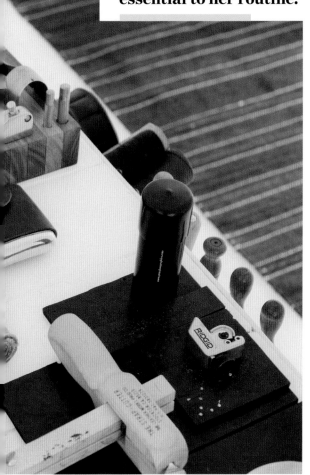

Material Matters

Much of Hannah's love for her craft lies in the ongoing challenge of coaxing new forms from the unique characteristics of each metal. Just as she uses a prescribed set of boundaries to structure her creativity, she has shaped the studio around the few natural materials essential to her routine. The worn wood handles of her rasps and awls set the tone for the weathered pine, ash, and oak tables that anchor the room. The faded nap of a buffing cloth also appears in a webbed-canvas seat back, a linen pin board, a braided-rope catchall. And, of course, the metals themselves—warm gold, bright silver, weighty bronze—inspire touches from the iron-pipe legs of a workbench to the aluminum cage of a fan, from a pair of brass scissors to the wire canister that holds them. In her decor as in her jewelry designs, variety arises not from a wide range of materials but from the unexpected ways that Hannah celebrates the elemental qualities of each.

Create with Coherence: How to Bring It Home

- Identify the steps in your creative process and devote an area of your room to each one. If space is limited, consider designating a different storage tote to each phase of the activity and keeping only one out at a time.

- A neutral palette and uncluttered surfaces can soothe a busy mind, even one that becomes easily distracted. Moreover, a simple, streamlined workspace is easier to keep clean for enhanced productivity!

- Whether your style is sleek and modern or rustic and timeworn, tactile surfaces anchor the senses more fully in the present and enhance creative flow—so put the focus on textural touches that suit your sensibility.

Create with Credibility

DIY Darling

A daughter raised among artists and engineers, crafters and carpenters, will likely learn a thing or two about creativity. Sure enough, Claire Zinnecker has not fallen far from her innovative family's tree. Claire remembers her childhood as one spent answering the question, "Why buy it if we can make it ourselves?" Though she took off her tool belt when she left home to earn an interior design degree, she quickly rediscovered her penchant for problem solving when she became a regular contributor for the popular lifestyle blog of her longtime friend and fellow Austin resident Camille Styles. Claire garnered a reputation—as well as an extensive online following—with the accessible appeal of her straightforward yet striking DIY ideas.

As the followers flooded in, so too did the inquiries for Claire's services. By the fall of 2013 she'd raised enough interest to launch her own firm for designing residential and commercial interiors. Yet she still reserves time in her busy schedule for the hands-on projects that keep her client designs fresh and her creative fires burning. Today, the 1940s bungalow that she shares with her pups, Monte and Emma, functions partly as a grounding home office, partly as an active construction zone, and entirely as a stunning playground for Claire's ingenuity.

The bungalow functions as a playground for ingenuity.

The gallery wall consists entirely of empty frames into which Claire tapes an ever-changing assortment of photos, artwork, and three-dimensional objects.

Built to Inspire

Whenever Claire spots a piece she loves in a shop or shelter magazine, she immediately sets her course to Home Depot for the components she needs to make a similar item herself. This DIY approach allows Claire not only to get her desired look on a budget but also to surround herself with constant reminders of her own resourcefulness. Lamps fabricated from wood and glass flank the sofa with their angular-meets-airy architecture. On the wall above the desk—itself a simple trestle-and-board unit that Claire assembled—two bands of untanned leather suspend a length of two-by-four for the most basic but beautiful shelf ever. Hand-poured concrete containers display succulents atop cement and copper-pipe plant stands; wire Acapulco chairs boast the cheerful custom touch of tightly wrapped pink twine; and even Monte and Emma benefit from their owner's handiwork each time they doze on a bed rendered one-of-a-kind by Claire's embroidery needle. Taken together, the handmade creations that fill the house testify to Claire's determination to solve any problem she sets her mind to.

It's All Relative

Claire fondly recalls the influence of the many loved ones who taught her the skills and mindset so integral to her current success. So, as much as possible, she incorporates into her home hand-me-downs from the relatives who imparted upon her the family passion for invention and imagination. She's installed as a focal point the Danish teak console that her grandfather (an actual rocket scientist!) lovingly maintained during the six decades it occupied his own residence. The handsome showpiece displays an oil portrait by Claire's uncle, mounted in a frame he mitered himself. A collection of birds inherited from her grandmother alight on surfaces throughout the space. Everywhere Claire turns, she's reminded of the creative heritage that has brought her to where she is today.

Detour by Design

As in any profession, Claire's projects sometimes hit a wall. Rather than charge through roadblocks, Claire has found that they frequently clear themselves if she sets her brain to idle and directs her attention to tasks that require a more mechanical skill set. She's therefore designed her home to facilitate impromptu mental diversions. In the living room, the lightweight IKEA coffee table and hide rug easily make way for large-scale tasks; and in the studio a pinboard and shelf of vignettes support explorations of color, texture, and proportion. Most notably, however, the gallery wall at her front door consists entirely of empty frames into which Claire tapes an ever-changing assortment of photos, artwork, and even three-dimensional objects. The frames lend order to the otherwise haphazard mix. And the overall flexibility gives Claire exactly what she needs: a workspace that can switch gears as often as she does.

Create with Credibility: How to Bring It Home

- DIY at least one decor element in your workspace. If large pieces like lighting and furnishings aren't up your alley, even something small such as a favorite quotation in your own hand can stand as a constant reminder of your ingenuity.

- Display photos or treasures of the family members, friends, and mentors who have influenced your creative journey. For example, you might display a pair of needles from the aunt who taught you to knit, or a framed letter of reference from the professor who encouraged your interest in writing poetry.

- Have an emergency plan for when your creativity stagnates, and design your space to invigorate it. Anything can replenish the creative well, from a shelf of old magazines for visual inspiration to a portion of wall left bare for impromptu yoga handstand sessions.

Create with Cunning

Draft and Edit

On the surface, writers have it easy. With only a pen and paper—or these days a decent laptop—they can work from anywhere. Yet as Chloe Roth will quickly point out, writers descend from temperamental stock. No household chore is too small, no ancillary conversation too boring, no leaky faucet too quiet to provide sufficient distraction and result in a dismal day's output. Chloe, never at a loss for words, has more than a few to say about distraction. For years she lived with as many as five roommates at a time, sacrificing her space and her sanity to pursue her dreams as a lyricist and music journalist. Yet as she neared thirty, she began to question the moving goalposts and monetary uncertainties of her chosen profession. She needed to shift gears.

That shift came in the form of a last-minute copywriting assignment Chloe took over for a friend. Though new to marketing, Chloe had a clever command of language that segued smoothly from songwriter to sloganeer. She soon found herself managing the branding and social media accounts of several up-and-coming brands—and craving a space of her own where she could transition from casual consultant to full-time freelancer. A grueling search of San Francisco's competitive real estate market led to a lease on a one-room apartment in the city's Castro District. Now, Chloe wrangles words in the peace and quiet of her sunlit studio, thankful for room to write at last.

THE VALLEY

AFA · THE NEW YORKER · SanFrancisco · 7

Guide to Grammar and Style

Like most writers, Chloe is also an avid reader and has amassed a considerable quantity of books over the years. However, the single room of her flat serves as her living, dining, and sleeping area as well as her office, leaving little room for a large shelving unit. Chloe gave up most of her library when she moved, but she wanted to retain a literary presence. Snippets of type therefore pepper the space. A wall-mounted rack displays periodicals selected as much for their bold mastheads as for their contents. Near the front door, a kaleidoscope of clippings and quotations greets guests with more than just hello. And as a nod to Chloe's Southern California birthplace, a hand-painted road sign points to "The Valley." Despite the absence of her beloved books, Chloe still honors the centrality of words in her work and in her life.

Just for Laughs

Chloe draws considerable delight from a sharp turn of phrase, a blistering bon mot, or even a groan-worthy pun. She has applied this keen wit to her decor as well, accenting her space with quirky, humorous finds. Above the sofa an R-rated diptych by a well-known local artist ensconces the room in its pillowy purple bosom. Business cards in a vintage stand read "Chloe Roth, Professional Hand Model," Chloe's tongue-in-cheek alter-ego career. Finally, several miniature midcentury desk lamps riff on typical task lighting, inducing smiles with their petite scale as well as their peculiar personalities. The humor that is Chloe's hallmark resonates throughout.

Sheer curtains distill a concentrated hit of sunlight.

Chloe has applied her keen wit to her decor, accenting the space with quirky, humorous finds.

Gift of the Tropics

To counteract the long, sometimes stifling hours she spends at her computer, Chloe has filled her apartment with elements that replicate the invigorating atmosphere of Hawaii—where she grew up and where she now frequently visits to recharge her creative engine. Sheer curtains distill a concentrated hit of sunlight from San Francisco's foggy skies and pour it onto the desk. On a nearby wooden clothes rack, Chloe recalls the brilliance of hothouse flowers with a rotating showcase of her most vivid attire. When she isn't tending her garden of shirts and shoes, she's greening her thumb with a jungle's worth of houseplants. The abundance of fragrance and foliage, color and light, simulate Chloe's tropical homeland to stimulate and inspire her.

Create with Cunning: How to Bring It Home

- Surround yourself with objects that remind you of why you have chosen your particular creative path. An avid reader and writer might frame illustrations from the books she loved as a child, while a graphic designer could collect and display unusual packaging from around the world.

- Creativity requires a healthy dash of humor, play, and spontaneity. Tell yourself to take it easy with decor that makes you smile, be it artwork or a tongue-in-cheek collection.

- Recall moments of your life when your creativity seemed to flow smoothly and easily. Remember where you were in space and time, and incorporate reminders of those moments into your interior for a "creative happy place" you can access 24/7.

DISCONNE

CT The
Bedroom

Nothing puts a shine on the world like a good, long vacation. At the beach we dig our toes into the sand and let the current carry away our cares. In a foreign city we step outside our comfort zone to find both fascination and familiarity in the tastes and traditions of other cultures. And regardless of our destination, we return home ready to dive back into life and paddle toward the new, broader horizons before us. Yet for more and more of us, due to work hours and budgetary constraints, vacations fall under the same "as-if" umbrella as the Tooth Fairy and flying cars.

With the hungry appetite of responsibility eating up our precious holiday hours, our domestic downtime has greater import than ever. Yet the external forces pressing on us now intrude upon our inner sanctums as well. Immediately upon waking we check email, Twitter, Instagram. Then we crawl out of bed. Go to work. Come home. Fall into bed. Watch TV. Check email, Twitter, Instagram. Drift off and dream about doing it all again tomorrow. Between Netflix for iPad and texting on the toilet, we've come a long way from the days when our private spaces provided respite from the outside world.

The mental suck of this virtual vacuum begets some serious IRL consequences. In the name of multitasking we switch from assessing the latest street style trends to addressing a coworker's after-hours request, from reviewing the kids' homework to reading the ratings on a replacement blender blade. An atmosphere of chaos prevails, one in which we're always racing to catch up and never completing any task to the best of our abilities. All the while, our attention spans decrease at a rate inversely proportional to our mounting stress levels. When we do grant ourselves a respite, a ceaselessly spinning subconscious and an itchy keypad thumb override our ability to enjoy the break.

Fortunately, it's never too late to pull the plug on the digital catch-22 and restore serenity to its rightful place: the bedroom. Every aspect of this space possesses a vacation's power to replenish our depleted stores. A sense of order and ease fosters a comfortable climate for reading and reflection. Layers such as plump pillows and luxurious linens calm the senses and defrazzle the nerves. Personal mementoes direct our thoughts inward, while visual elements exemplify the emotional abstractions that thoughtful design can make very real: hues that soothe, lighting that uplifts, proportion that slows the eye and relaxes the mind. Each of us can find the formula to make the bedroom a place where we'll automatically leave the phone at the door—and a place from which we'll emerge refreshed.

Each of us has a different recipe for relaxation. What are the ingredients in yours? Which activities would you most like to encourage in the bedroom? Would firmer pillows or an upholstered headboard be conducive to propping yourself up in bed with a good book every night? Or does reading in bed put you straight to sleep and would a comfy corner chair suit you better? What quality of light makes you feel most calm: moody and reflective or bright and glowing? Finally, what can you eliminate from the space to make it feel like a sanctuary from the stresses of the outside world? For example, if a nightstand makes it hard to resist charging your phone there and checking it immediately upon waking, you might skip a bedside table in favor of just a wall-mounted sconce. After all, removing stressful activities from your bedroom has as much of an impact as reinforcing calming ones.

This chapter introduces four busy individuals who hit the brakes when they found themselves riding a one-way train to burnout. They include an artist and antiques expert who replicated the indulgent style of her favorite boutique hotels in her own home; a shop owner who brought to life her enduring love of literature to help her weather the vagaries of her prolonged transitional state; a stylist who redrew the boundaries of privacy when she decided to sleep in her living room; and an interior designer who created a bedroom that's neither quiet nor conventional but that still provides exactly the escape she needs at the end of the day. Taken collectively, their spaces illustrate that no matter how small our homes or how hectic our schedules, we can take back tranquility—one bedroom at a time.

Disconnect with Pleasure

Inherent Style

Among life's most memorable occasions, the mother-daughter getaway ranks supreme. Christine Flynn cites countless childhood expeditions with her mom as the determining factor in her eye for antiques and her addiction to the hunt. The two foraged flea markets far and wide, indulging along the way in life's little luxuries and in thoughts of one day owning a store together. And when her mother passed away, Christine channeled that intent and opened Love the Design. The decor boutique quickly became a mainstay in Toronto's shopping scene, fueled by Christine's tireless quest for the ultimate vintage find.

Today, Christine counts the store as just one of many enterprises that keep her on her toes; a fine arts photography practice, as well as a husband and two sons, make those mother-daughter escapades seem distant indeed. So, upon her family's recent move to a new house, Christine seized the opportunity to furnish her bedroom in the cosmopolitan character that marks the world's great hotels. She called upon her own inventory as well as her impeccable instinct for interiors to fashion a personal retreat that whispers of freshly washed robes and room-service trays—and of which her mom would have approved wholeheartedly.

Decadent Dreams

As any traveler who has ever tossed aside luggage and flopped onto a mint-bedecked pillow can relate, nothing beats the deep sigh of release that accompanies arrival at a destination. Christine has captured and amplified the fleeting ecstasy of that moment with the layered textiles and luxe touches in her bedroom. She and her husband sleep each night in a linen-upholstered bed, resting atop an extra-deep mattress and beneath a sateen duvet and cashmere throw. Metallic accents, from the nails on the tufted headboard to the filament of an Edison bulb, glimmer in sunlight and moonlight alike. Unless, of course, Christine has closed the silk curtains to let the crystal chandelier suspended from the ceiling cast its opulent glow. The scene beckons with all the amenity of a presidential suite.

Just Add Patina

In line with her preference for the timeworn allure of antiques, Christine finds herself drawn to the sense of history that marks her favorite places. To evoke the old-world depth of cities such as Paris and London, Christine mixed weathered industrial accents into the bedroom's luxurious setting. Metal surfaces throughout have a tarnished, rather than polished, finish. Reclaimed marble and iron nightstands flank the bed, one hosting a shadeless brass lamp while the other moors the exposed bulb of a caged pendant light. A salvaged wood cash-register drawer sorts accessories on the bureau, a corner chair showcases a denim quilt that belonged to Christine's mother, and a pair of antelope skulls watches over it all. In lieu of a store-bought sensibility, Christine has created a space that appears to have coalesced over time and that feels the richer for it.

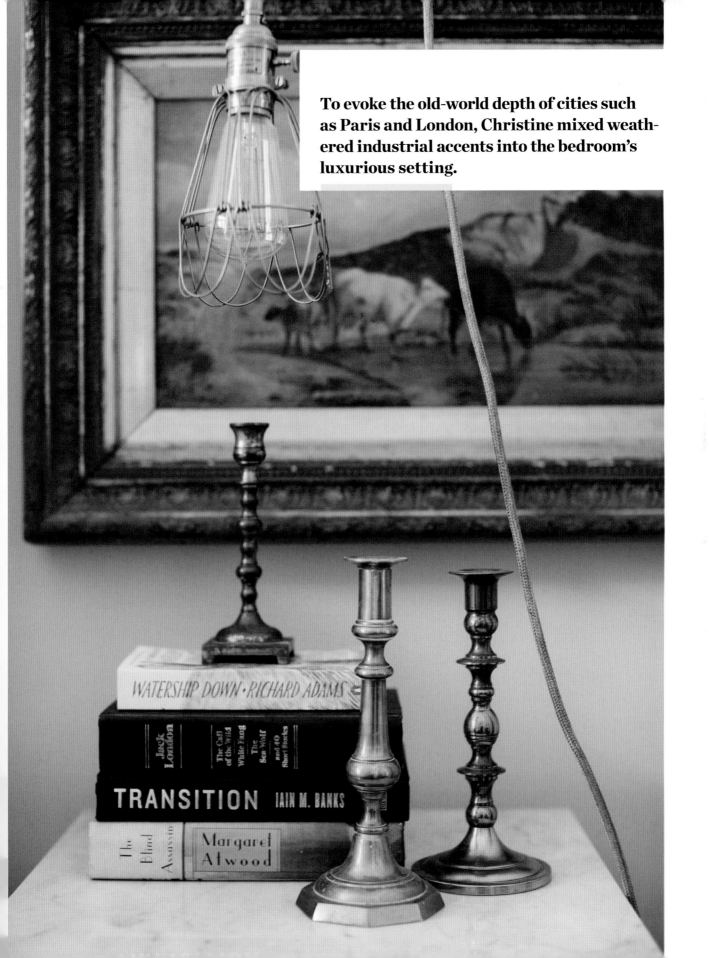

To evoke the old-world depth of cities such as Paris and London, Christine mixed weathered industrial accents into the bedroom's luxurious setting.

Grand and Graceful

To complete her lavish, feminine aesthetic, Christine has installed an art and accessories arrangement reminiscent of the palaces and portrait galleries of Europe. Her collection of female nudes could just as easily be on loan from a nineteenth-century Parisian atelier as it could be her own accumulation. Mirrors mixed in with the drawings and photos add a reflective dimension. Finally, jewelry from around the globe enhances the display, the gemstones and precious metals complementing the gilt frames that offset each piece. Whether she's rushing to work or lounging with coffee and the paper, Christine starts each day surrounded by the pieces and memories she treasures most.

Disconnect with Pleasure: How to Bring It Home

- Mimic the indulgences of hotel living in your own bedroom. Mount a hook for a plush robe behind the door, add two extra pillows to the mix for sitting up and reading in bed, and seek out no-wrinkle sheets for that crisp hotel feel.

- A sense of age can make the difference between a bedroom that feels too contrived for comfort and one that feels inviting and lived-in. Balance a luxe space with patined surfaces, frayed textiles, and industrial details.

- Rather than hide favorite fashion pieces in the closet, incorporate them into your decor. Put an entire collection on display, such as jewelry in a compartmentalized tray on the dresser, or an especially striking silk scarf draped over the bedpost.

Disconnect with Patience

Choose Your Own Adventure

Nothing rivals a good book for the ultimate escape. During a peripatetic childhood, Mary Spears often turned to the solace and companionship of her favorite novels as her family's constant relocation made lasting friendships difficult. In her twenties, she held them closer while she traveled the world for an international nonprofit. Most recently, in the face of her last-minute acceptance to a master's program for literature, Mary and her husband, Will, abandoned nearly everything in their sprawling Georgia farmhouse to start anew in a tiny Boston flat. Everything, that is, except their books.

Mary also carried with her a penchant for vintage, honed over a lifetime of thrifting and heightened by an avid reader's fascination with the past lives of objects. When her casual hobby selling antique clothing online flourished into a viable business, Mary quit her graduate degree and devoted herself full-time to the shop. And when her growing mountains of merchandise conspired with Will's med school materials to consume the couple's entire apartment, Mary cordoned off the bedroom and looked to her love of reading to inspire its design. Now, with yet another move for Will's studies on the horizon, Mary pauses gratefully in a familiar yet refreshing space that dog-ears this chapter in the unfolding story of her life.

Like a writer compiling disparate scenes into a novel, Mary structures her small decor elements into succinctly composed vignettes.

Narrative Ark

To create stability in a sea of uncertainty, Mary has furnished her interior exclusively with thrifted, scavenged, and hand-me-down items. For just as a detailed backstory brings a character to life, pre-loved finds ground the bedroom in time and space. Each piece tells a tale of its origins and also of how it came to be in Mary and Will's possession. A wrought-iron bed from the 1940s made its first home in a small fishing village and required a day's drive up the coast to retrieve. A chinoiserie dressing screen was picked up for twenty dollars at a yard sale, with amusing anecdotes about the previous owner thrown in for free. The antique vanity mirror is a relic of Mary's childhood, for years one of her mother's most prized items. Whenever Mary feels adrift, a glance at her biography of objects anchors her.

Tight Tableaux

Mary readily admits that a vintage aesthetic can become jumbled and heavy-handed. So like a writer compiling disparate scenes into a novel, Mary structures her small decor elements into succinctly composed vignettes. Each setting offers the eye a distinct moment of rest and interest. Antique brooches and bracelets dialogue in a glass jewelry case atop the dresser. A lace doily and an ostrich feather drape a stack of hardcover books for a bedside exposition on supple and substantial. Next to the window, a velvet fedora caps the folding screen and flirts with a bare burlap hat form on the table below. Into every arrangement, Mary incorporates fresh flowers, highlighting only one variety of blossom at a time to strike a note both organic and ordered. With her skillful edit, Mary keeps the fussiness factor at bay while still giving each object its due.

A skillful edit keeps fussiness at bay.

Blank Pages

Overall, a remarkable austerity defines Mary and Will's bedroom. The stark aesthetic not only echoes the spare yet expressive language of the authors on Mary's shelves—Dickinson, Woolf, Millay—it also reflects the couple's determination to dwell peacefully in the unknowns of their transitional state. To keep belongings at a minimum for future moves, and to exploit the evocative energy of negative space, they pared down their large furnishings to only the barest essentials of a bed, a chest of drawers, a nightstand, and a chair. Continuing their minimalist approach, they used the apartment's existing white walls as the basis for a monochromatic landscape comprised of a white wrought-iron bed, white blankets and sheets, and gossamer white curtains. What little color does appear, via small decor and accessories, has the faded and timeworn quality of laundry left overlong in the sun. The room emanates the mystery of a space abandoned decades before, and hums with the potential of an unfinished sentence waiting for Mary and Will to step in and complete it.

Disconnect with Patience: How to Bring It Home

- Learn the history of each object in your space for a greater sense of groundedness within the whole. Vintage finds work best for this, but even a new item has a story worth imagining: the path it took to reach the store, the life of the shop employee who placed it on the shelf.

- Approach styling your small decor as though you're writing a haiku. Establish rules for each arrangement—for example, choose three objects of different heights, each of a different material but all of the same color—and find ways to create interest within that structure.

- Make your bedroom a retreat that feels removed from place and time with antiqued colors, textiles, and surface treatments. Think sun-bleached whites and heathered blues, over-washed linens and faded florals, or crackling paint and tarnished mirrors.

Disconnect with Peace

Internal Dilemma

To dispel the commonly but erroneously held myth that an introvert is by nature antisocial, look no further than Julie Pointer. The stylist and art director has spent the last several years managing the events division of the highly esteemed food and entertaining publication *Kinfolk*. Indeed, she even earned a graduate degree in experience design and has assiduously applied it to the block parties and holiday dinners she hosts for her neighbors and friends. Yet Julie is also the first to admit that for every minute spent in the presence of others, she craves ten on her own. For as much as she thrives on company, Julie has learned that her energy stores can only be replenished in solitude.

Julie didn't arrive at this realization easily and met it at first with resistance. Yet after several seasons of growing increasingly depleted by the gamut of gatherings she produced and attended for work, Julie accepted that in order to pour herself fully into her collaborative endeavors, she needed space and time to refill her own cup. She has created the former in her Portland, Oregon, studio apartment, and now she reserves plenty of the latter among the rustic and restful touches that define her home.

Julie put her bed in the living room to take advantage of the natural light that streams through the large bay windows.

Lounge Layout

The biggest challenge Julie encountered in establishing a personal retreat lay in the limited square footage of her apartment. Although the unit does have a small second room, it has no window and can accommodate nothing larger than a twin mattress—an atmosphere more bleak than beneficial. Rather than settle for the cramped nook, Julie put her bed in the living room to take advantage of the natural light that streams through the large bay windows. Granted, she had initial reservations about having her bedroom open to guests, but she's since discovered that the arrangement disarms visitors and elicits from them the same uninhibited attitude she herself adopts in her space. Julie describes the dynamic as a study in psychology, a glimpse at the power of design to make people more comfortable with vulnerability, and an experience that has allowed her to explore the spectrum of privacy for herself.

Applied Decompression

Julie points out that although she's not always "actively unwinding" when she's home, the presence of the bed makes everything she does in her home feel more restorative. When she's not reclining with a book, she's reading with her legs tucked up in the corner chair. A desk facilitates journaling and sketching, as well as creating the collages that Julie turns to when she seeks the solace of her fine arts background. The choice to place her bed in the middle of the apartment gives Julie the leeway she desires to practice a range of relaxing activities in the same space as where she sleeps.

Ephemeral objects promote a sense of Zen nonattachment.

Finding Zen

From the rising mist on a lake at dawn to the slow slide of the setting sun, Julie derives considerable peace from the unhurried progress of the natural world. She's sourced most of her decor from the wilderness to evoke the same steady calm. Bundles of twigs and driftwood recall the quiet majesty of the tree line where forest meets shore. Handmade clay vases hold dried flowers and berries rescued from the photo shoots Julie has styled. Depending on the season and on Julie's whim, a handful of peppercorns may spill from a basket, a stump may pose as a stool, or tumbleweeds may cluster in a corner. The ephemeral quality of each object engenders in Julie a sense of Zen nonattachment. As each treasure disintegrates and makes way for something else, Julie is reminded of precisely what she has come here to do: let it all go.

Disconnect with Peace: How to Bring It Home

◆ Invite friends into your bedroom when they visit: the calming, disarming effect it has on both hostess and guest might surprise and delight you both.

◆ Space devoted to your favorite reflective activities means one less obstacle to actually doing them. A comfortable chair with adequate lighting promotes pre-bed reading, while a corner floor cushion supports that morning meditation practice you've been meaning to start.

◆ Found natural objects add a layer of personal interest without feeling too precious or contrived. Reserve a bowl on your dresser for an assortment of interesting stones, tuck a collection of feathers between your mirror and its frame, and don't think twice about switching it up when you're ready for something new!

Disconnect with Panache

Occupational Hazard

Just as doctors make the worst patients, interior designers make their own worst clients. After all, no one likes to bring her job home at the end of the day. Yet as Bay Area interiors expert Susie Ho knows all too well, a designer's work often involves as much cat herding and hand-holding as it does space planning and product sourcing, making quality downtime all the more essential. Susie first gained exposure to the ins and outs of the interiors industry during her years as a senior designer at a high-end firm. Yet it wasn't until she left the corporate world to focus on smaller residential work that the diplomacy of managing clients began to combine with the demands of running her own business to leave her feeling constantly drained. As Susie's project roster grew, so did the stress on her psyche and her desire to recharge.

A move from Los Angeles to San Francisco for her husband's work provided Susie the perfect excuse to carve out a personal retreat. In contrast to the open-concept loft she'd left behind, her new apartment offered all the intimate charm of its prewar origins. Susie appointed the tiny but inviting bedroom using her signature vintage-with-a-twist style, as well as the many designer tricks she keeps up her sleeve. The finished result employs plenty of character and even a little magic to give Susie exactly what she needed most: a place to catch her breath.

Dark walls emphasize the plush, inviting nature of the bed.

The dark walls diffuse the light that enters the windows for a subtly radiant atmosphere.

Scene Stealer

Because Susie often has to rein in her tastes to satisfy the safer visions of clients, creating a space uniquely her own meant giving free run to her more adventurous design inclinations. Her decorative indulgence took the form of a 1970s padded headboard upholstered in plush velvet. Scavenged on Craigslist, the bed boasts a commanding presence with its midnight blue hue and over-the-top Studio 54 vibe. To prevent the piece from feeling like a non sequitur, Susie gave it context with a vibrant mix of smaller but similarly quirky elements; a beaded macramé plant hanger, green ikat curtains, and tropical-print throw pillows complement the headboard's flamboyance without overpowering the room altogether. The bed and its decorative "wingmen" leave little question that Susie has staked the space as her own.

Inner Glow

Rather than lament the bedroom's diminutive size, Susie opted to emphasize its small scale for an intimate sensibility. She first applied a coat of inky blue paint that matches the headboard. The dark walls not only emphasize the plush, inviting nature of the bed, they also diffuse the light that enters the west-facing windows for a subtly radiant atmosphere in the late afternoon—the time of day when Susie most often finds herself retreating to the space. The curtains, though colorful, are sheer enough to filter the sun for added softness. Susie left the walls above the picture-rail molding white, creating a layer of dimension that both emphasizes the room's height and emulates the cloistered effect of coffered ceilings. The room shelters its occupants like a jewel box protecting its cache.

Keep It In Check

To offset the drama of the room's centerpiece and envelope, Susie selected finishing accents that balance the room with their understated scale and finish. Bedside tables made from live edge oak supply organic contrast and display equally earthy curios of wood and glass. A matelassé bedspread in crisp ecru provides a tailored touch. Finally, twin task lamps of powder-coated steel frame the extravagant headboard in spare, utilitarian precision. The mix of eccentricity and restraint surrounds Susie with a sense of composed equilibrium so that she can restore her own.

Disconnect with Panache: How to Bring It Home

- A bedroom needn't have quiet decor to offer a restful escape. Sometimes the mere act of filling a space with personality-packed items that speak exactly to your stylistic sensibility is enough to make it feel like a personal haven.

- Embrace the dimensions of a small bedroom by employing a moody palette and atmospheric lighting to transform

what space you *do* have into a sheltered retreat. Keep colors in the same family for a dynamic yet cohesive effect.

- Natural elements can add an organic touch to a highly stylized space without detracting from the drama. An overgrown hanging plant, bold wood grain, and floral-print linens all hold their own among statement-making furnishings and decor.

GROW

The Kids' Room

L ace-bedecked canopy beds, pastel walls plastered in glossy magazine clippings, books and dolls vying for shelf space with abandoned rock collections, crumbled party favors, and inexplicably precious vending-machine prizes. As with the fashions of decades past, most of us look back at our childhood decor with a mix of fondness and bemused chagrin. With jumbled closets or questionable color palettes, our rooms may not have represented the pinnacle of order or style, but they gave us the space we needed to put our first stamp on the world.

Just as any teacher will emphasize the importance of classroom setup for a smooth, productive school day with absorbed, enthusiastic students, parents can design their children's rooms with an eye toward crafting a growth-minded environment. The right mix of essentials and extras, structure and independence, can strike that delicate balance between allowing little ones the freedom to grow as individuals and providing the stability and routine so critical to their developing minds. Given the responsibilities that rest on the shoulders of all caregivers, who among us couldn't use some assistance facilitating the fun of playtime, the discipline of tidy-up time, the quiet of bedtime?

Yet in the course of decorating a kid's space, the path invariably leads to a crossroads at which adult wisdom and youthful whimsy clash. The colors and materials deemed age appropriate for babies and children often yield an aesthetic more garish than engaging. Crayons, markers, and paints seem to self-replicate at an exponential pace, threatening to consume the whole room—as well as anyone who dares impose control over the chaos. And when at last a space has achieved a happy equilibrium, its young occupant sprouts up five inches, discards previous hobbies for fascinating new ones, and fits the formerly fantastic room about as well as last summer's swimsuit. Parents throw up their hands in the ongoing quest for kids' rooms that are at once fun, functional, and friendly on the eyes.

But like the cloud that requires only imagination to become a pirate ship traversing the sky, a troublesome interior acquires infinite potential when viewed with the wonder and curiosity of the young. So look no further than the library or the local ice cream parlor to inspire decor that delights. Toss the growth chart and instead apply the timeless tenets of design for colors that calm, textures that beckon, and furnishings that adapt from toddler to teen. Draw outside the lines to create a space that exhibits the same unbounded confidence you want to instill in your offspring.

There are several factors to consider when approaching the design of your child's room. Take into account not only a child's current age but how long you'd like the room to suit them without a major overhaul. Gender can also influence design, though of course you needn't stick to the old pink and blue scripts if other palettes appeal to you more. Most important, however, are questions of balance and compromise. To what extent would you like the space to feel cohesive with the rest of the house while still maintaining its own personality? How many hours a day will your child spend in the room, and how should they be apportioned for play, learning, and rest? How can this space be one that honors both your tastes and their desires? Though the answers to these questions may shift over the years, an enduring interior can evolve with them.

The solutions for kids' rooms are as one-of-a-kind as the children who inhabit them. We'll meet a Minnesota couple who have ensconced their infant daughter in a soothing sensorial haven; a former teacher who put her training to work for a bedroom that both educates and enthralls her active son; a pair of Pasadena parents who, in the wake of a life-altering diagnosis, transformed their dining room into a full-time classroom so they could homeschool their elementary-aged trio; and an events stylist who helped her two preteens explore their emerging personalities by plumbing her own vast warehouse of vintage finds. We'll see how these moms and dads have used decor as they would any other parenting tool, and in so doing have given the whole family a place to learn, play, rest, and repeat.

Grow Tenderly

Return to Eden

Tales of young love and small-town charm rarely occur outside the realm of fiction. However, the script-worthy romance of Max and Johnna Holmgren is 100 percent fact. The couple, who met in the seventh grade, pinpoint the nascence of their relationship to historic Stillwater, Minnesota; the community's picturesque Main Street marked the halfway point between Max and Johnna's respective hometowns and therefore witnessed many a milkshake date in their budding relationship. Several years and a marriage ceremony later, the sweethearts heeded the big-city call of nearby Minneapolis. Yet before long, the impending arrival of daughter Luella propelled Max and Johnna back to Stillwater with the goal of giving their child the same idyllic upbringing that had left its mark on them.

Though evenings now find the trio strolling down tree-lined streets to the ice cream parlor, a challenge lies in maintaining similar calm during the day. Max and Johnna run a design business from home and apportion their time so two-year-old Lu always has at least one parent present. To avoid a chaotic tag-team atmosphere, they've situated the toddler's room on the ground level and the office upstairs where a second bedroom would be. The somewhat unconventional arrangement allows for focused work—and, more importantly, for uninterrupted periods of play in a space devoted to slowing down and noticing the little things.

The room thrums with the wholesome simplicity of childhoods past.

The arrangement allows for uninterrupted periods of play in a space devoted to slowing down and noticing the little things.

Tiny Relics

The Holmgrens subscribe to a style of parenting that encourages Luella to learn at her own pace through self-directed observation and exploration. With this approach in mind, they've decorated her room to stimulate even as it soothes. The faded and timeworn charm of vintage furnishings characterizes the room's larger pieces, including the oak roll-top desk and tin-framed chalkboard. Smaller elements, such as the polka-dot curtains and the gallery wall of carved wood objects, focus more on strong shapes and patterns than on saturated hues. What little color does appear in the space takes its cues from the muted quality of the vintage safety sign and botanical teaching chart. The room hums with the wholesome simplicity of childhoods past.

Castle in the Clouds

Max and Johnna have eschewed toys with lights, screens, or mechanical parts, instead supplying Luella with objects that foster interactive play. To enhance this emphasis on lo-fi sensory engagement, they've incorporated accents that feature a variety of textures for maximum tactile stimulation. High-pile furs and hides blanket the hardwood floors, laying a fuzzy foundation for indoor picnics. Mounded burrows of heathered quilts and crocheted afghans dot the room. Finally, in a flash of inspiration, Johnna elicited an easier ride from the wood rocking horse by swaddling its seat with a knit scarf from her own wardrobe. A gentle touch guides every moment from nap time to story time and beyond.

Hideaway Haven

As parents, the Holmgrens have charged themselves with instilling in Luella the confidence that comes with a sense of security. In order to fashion a child-appropriate sanctuary from the expanse of her room, they parceled it into nooks and crannies that Luella can easily access herself. Crawl into an oversized storage basket for a game of peek-a-boo, or flip it for an instant fort. Snuggle on the partially enclosed daybed, which Max created when he lowered the outgrown crib and left three of its four sides intact. And if Luella falls mysteriously silent, find her sleeping in the tee-pee that Johnna raised from vintage afghans and discarded lumber. With a few thoughtful decor elements, the couple has imposed cozy boundaries for an environment as safe and familiar as their own arms.

Grow Tenderly: How to Bring It Home

• When it comes to kids' spaces, interesting and engaging doesn't have to equal loud. The same classic patterns that appeal to you as an adult—a tonal polka dot, a subtle stripe—add a layer of fun and visual interest without feeling garish.

• Children are highly attuned to sensory input, so stimulate them with a variety of intriguing yet gentle textures. Fuzzy and fluffy, smooth or bumpy: it's all fair game!

• To help kids feel cozy and safe, fill their rooms with opportunities to create a space within a space. Large, lightweight storage bins are easy to overturn for an impromptu fort, and a clothesline that stretches across the room is just a blanket away from being a tent.

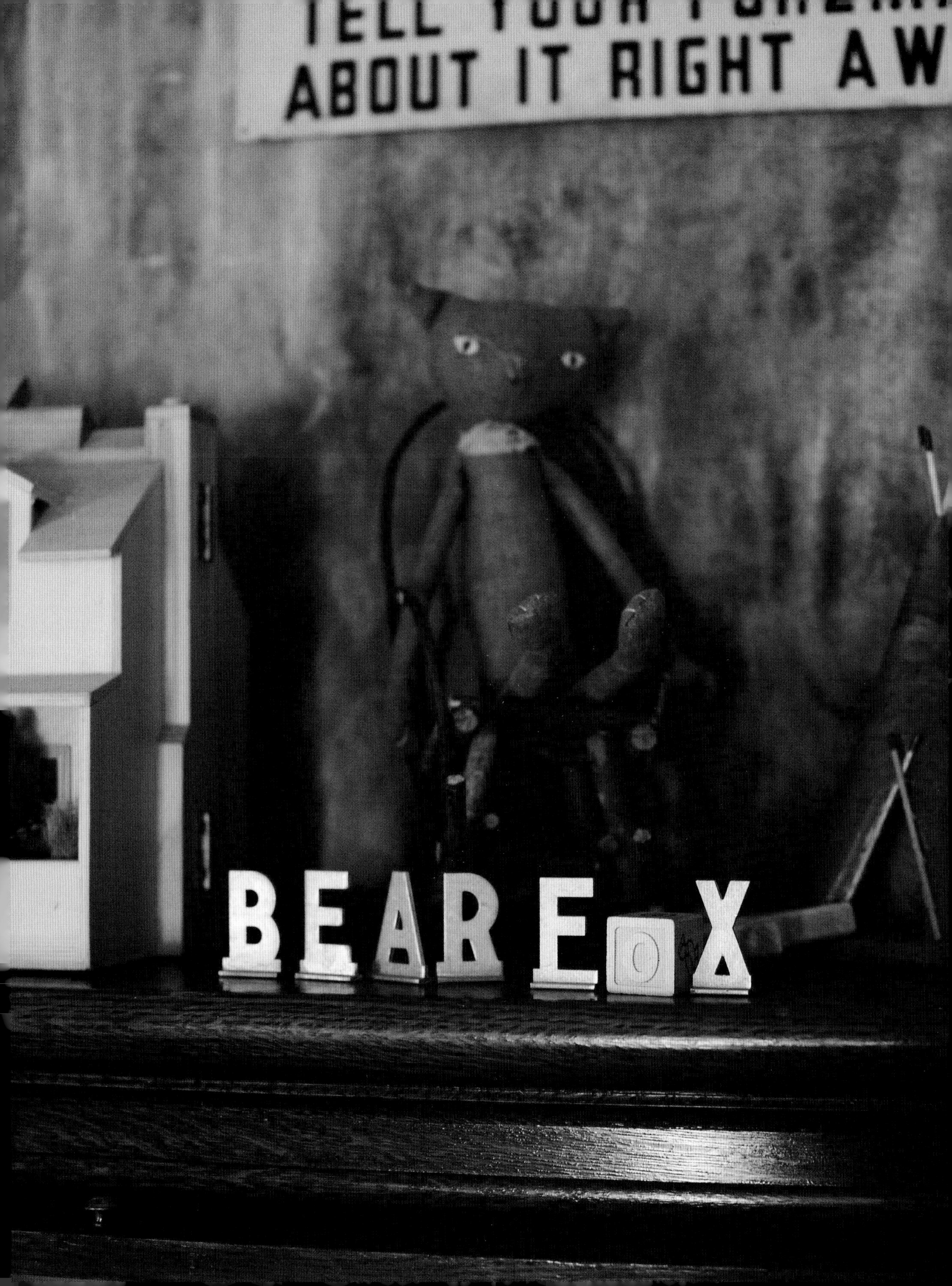
ABOUT IT RIGHT AW
BEAREOX

Grow Thoughtfully

Storied Tradition

Oxford, Mississippi, is an unlikely but legendary hitching post on the highway of the American imagination. For decades the community's thriving literary scene has attracted established and aspiring authors alike, among them Erin Abbott Kirkpatrick's mother. Erin recalls the constant stream of lectures, plays, and festivals that allied with Oxford's sleepy Southern charm to give her a childhood both stimulating and steady. The town's appealing dichotomy lived in Erin's mind long after her family moved away; remained there as she earned a degree in early childhood education; lingered for ten years while she toured the country nannying the offspring of several high-profile entertainers; and ultimately inspired her purchase of a rambling farmhouse just outside Oxford city limits. There Erin established a home base and continued her extensive travels until 2009, when the fading allure of the road settled her for good.

Erin soon entrenched herself more deeply in the community with the launch of Amelia, a boutique that highlights unique finds from independent artisans and that has since become wildly popular. Not long afterward, she and her husband welcomed their son, Tom Otis—along with the privilege of raising their child in the town Erin holds so dear. In decorating Tom's bedroom, Erin drew upon her background in education and her own idyllic Oxford memories to encourage both active adventures and wandering daydreams. The cheerful, engaging space combines equal parts enrichment and enchantment for a room in which the whole family can learn, dream, and grow together.

Education Stations

Erin follows the teachings of the Montessori tradition, which suggests that a child's play should foster a sense of freedom and independence within a prescribed set of limits. She drew from this perspective to determine the layout of Tom's room. Several distinct zones punctuate the perimeter, each offering a different type of pastime and each positioned so Tom can access it without assistance. Blocks pile high in braided-rope baskets beneath the window for hands-on fun. A canvas hamper keeps a drum, xylophone, and other wood instruments handy for Tom's frequent urge to strike up the band. Crayons and chalk live in wide-mouthed jars that rub shoulders with a pint-sized easel and its seemingly endless roll of paper. Erin defines each area according to its container so that Tom knows exactly where to reach for the activity of his choice—and also exactly where to return it before he moves on.

Now and Later

Many elements in Tom's room seem at first glance beyond the toddler's years. Yet Erin has intentionally incorporated precious objects into the mix, giving Tom's as yet unlearned abilities a chance to emerge. A one-of-a-kind globe lamp, with its delicate on-off switch, provides a lesson in treating belongings carefully. A vintage picnic table stands too high for Tom so currently displays toys and games, while its bench functions beautifully as a play surface until Tom can reach the table itself. Finally, a colorful assortment of books from Erin's own childhood, many of them signed by their authors and therefore irreplaceable, line a top shelf while newer offerings rest below. The signed volumes have taught Tom that all books require a gentle hand, and that these books in particular require Mom or Dad's hands for now. By viewing decor as an opportunity to teach and empower Tom in the world of adults, Erin has created a space that will age along with him.

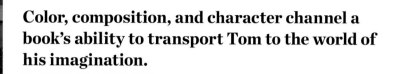

Color, composition, and character channel a book's ability to transport Tom to the world of his imagination.

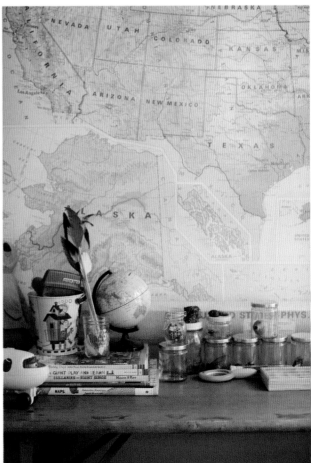

Grow Thoughtfully: How to Bring It Home

- Keep toys and belongings in check by establishing a straightforward organization system that kids can take part in maintaining. Categorize bins and baskets according to object type, and make cleanup a part of playtime to teach both sorting skills and a sense of responsibility.

- Resist the temptation to populate the space with kids-only furnishings and decor. Incorporate "grown-up" pieces where appropriate and use them to teach lessons in being careful or politely asking for help.

- Look to the schoolroom for decor inspiration. Faded primary colors, retro alphabet artwork, and classic picture book characters feel lighthearted and playful yet tasteful too—and they mesh nicely with a home that has a found vintage sensibility throughout.

Elementary Accents

When Tom beds down for the night, he does so in a picture book brought to life, for the hallmarks of children's literature have directly informed the room's decor. The saturated reds, blues, greens, and yellows that punctuate the room echo the rainbow of spines that fill Tom's shelves. Shapes from the chunky limbs of jointed animals to the printed triangles on a storage bin echo a kindergarten primer's bold, eye-catching appeal. Finally, framed animal and alphabet artworks feel borrowed from a library of illustrated classics. Color, composition, and character channel a book's ability to transport Tom to the world of his imagination long before he sounds out his first word.

Grow Thankfully

Resilience Rules

An abiding love of travel tops the list of shared qualities that first drew Brian and Nada Jones together. The couple spent the early years of their marriage crossing a host of exotic destinations from their list, and when they grew their number to include a daughter and two sons, they took it as a given that a lifetime of family expeditions stood before them. Then Brian received a diagnosis for a neuromuscular disease that would soon begin to affect his mobility and with it his ability to add new stamps to his passport. Suddenly, the future looked very different from what the Joneses had envisioned.

But Brian and Nada also have in common a no-regrets approach to life, so they decided the whole family would spend the next twelve months on the road together. Nada put her career as a women's entrepreneurship educator on hold so she could homeschool Sophia, Jack, and Asher (then nine, seven, and four, respectively). The breakfast nook in their Pasadena home became the trio's classroom, with the nation's parks and monuments their field-trip destinations. Though the family's year of adventure has now ended and the kids have returned to school, the room's design remains the same—making it the perfect place to sit down with homework, to look back without regrets, and to look forward to all that's still in store.

A for Adaptable

The transformation of dining room to schoolroom presented the challenge of accommodating three different grade levels. To leave latitude for the room to evolve along with the kids' needs, Nada furnished it simply and sparingly. A lightweight table from IKEA stands on wheels in the middle of the room. Large enough for all three children to gather for a lesson with Mom, yet small enough to be pushed aside for projects requiring more room, it provides a flexible work surface for simultaneous completion of individual assignments. A coat of chalkboard paint transforms every square inch of wall into a platform for practice sums and progress reports, and also eliminates the risks of hanging a heavy framed blackboard on the home's aging walls. Partway through the year, Nada added a corner-mounted TV to the space. In concert with a wireless mouse and keyboard, the unit provides streaming access to online teaching aides without the added bulk of a computer. As the kids grow and Sophia enters middle school, the room's potential will continue to reveal itself.

Age of Maturity

Because the room occupies a central location adjacent to the family's entryway and kitchen, Nada cultivated an overall aesthetic that, while youthful, also boasts a sophistication that meshes with the rest of her decor. The chalkboard walls, functional as they are, contribute to a high-contrast color scheme that includes the black molded-wood chairs, white shelving, and checkered linoleum floor. Gray-and-white chevron curtains add a dash of pattern that complements the palette. Furnishings, though scaled for young people, have a modern shape that any adult would appreciate. And finally, a blown-glass globe pendant hovers over the table with radiant aplomb. The room's crisp, graphic elements yield an all-ages design that blends seamlessly into the family's home.

Class Party

Throughout the year of homeschooling and now in the aftermath, the Joneses have viewed the classroom as a physical embodiment of their determination to turn obstacles into opportunities. As such, they've packed it with touches that reflect the same positivity. Nada encouraged the kids to draw, paint, and papier-mâché vibrant artwork that she then displayed in the built-in china hutches. Oversized Mason jars in the same cabinets offer up craft supplies and a sense of possibility. And a spunky wire bowl in fun fire-engine red holds seasonal arrangements of fruits, flowers, or souvenirs from the road. The resulting celebratory tone feels as spirited as the Joneses' past and as bright as their future.

Grow Thankfully: How to Bring It Home

- For a space that satisfies everyone, combine kid-friendly function with adult-friendly form. Simple, uncomplicated furnishings foster a distraction-free environment so kids can let their imaginations run wild, and also fit right in with the rest of a home's interior no matter what its style.

- Use decor to reinforce learning. Hang maps or historical photos in preparation for upcoming family trips; go on a scavenger hunt for tiny treasures of all one color and mount them in a shadow box; nurture succulent clippings and watch them grow.

- Flexible, multipurpose pieces not only offer versatility now, they help a space evolve as children grow. Telescoping legs allow tables and stools to get taller as kids do, and bulletin boards or even clipboards mounted on the wall allow art to be swapped in and out at will.

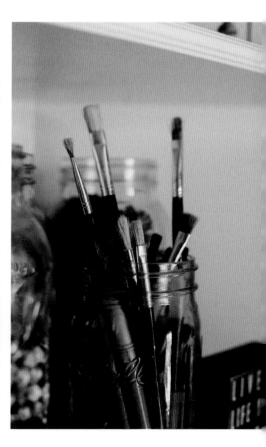

Grow Together

Spreading Their Wings

Jeni Maus is something of a decor alchemist. She routinely creates elaborate interiors settings where an empty field stood only moments before; and with her company, Found Vintage Rentals, she almost single-handedly launched the phenomenon of one-of-a-kind furniture vignettes as wedding and party decor. Brides and event planners clamber for access to Jeni's warehouse of vintage and refurbished finds, coveting her spot-on style as much as her prolific inventory. So, naturally, Jeni has always enjoyed taking charge of decorating the house she lives in with her husband, Joel, and their children, Bailey and Caysen.

For a decade the family slept in the attic rooms of their Southern California home, with Mom and Dad in one room and brother and sister sharing another—and with Jeni reigning over the look of it all. But as the kids approached their teen years, their desire to have individual bedrooms mounted. So Jeni and Joel relocated to the spare room downstairs and left the attic to the kids. The following months saw Jeni straddling the line between decor maven and mom as she helped thirteen-year-old Bailey and eleven-year-old Caysen fashion spaces that convey their developing identities through the language of design.

Railway Station
Hopwood Lane
Town Centre

Convey developing identities through the language of design.

Wherever possible, Jeni identified ways to overlap her taste with her kids' desires.

Vested Interest

Though Jeni could easily have delved into her giant trove of vintage treasures to furnish the kids' rooms, she wanted each to enjoy the self-esteem boost of receiving just-for-them items rather than hand-me-downs. Yet she thought it just as critical to impart her appreciation for the personality that vintage and handmade items bring to a space. So Jeni worked with the children to assemble Pinterest boards that captured the aesthetic they wanted, then helped them slowly over time to get the look. Weekends had them combing area flea markets, gathering supplies at the nursery for planting glass terrariums, and even reupholstering items from their old rooms to suit their new styles. With each project, Bailey's and Caysen's confidence mounted, leaving them fully invested in rooms that are every inch their own.

Yours, Mine, Ours

Wherever possible, Jeni identified ways to overlap her taste with her kids' desires. Most notably, shiplap siding now lines the walls throughout the attic. Jeni had long focused her eye on the shiplap as a means to inject the attic with her preferred rustic vibe, but Caysen and Bailey remained unconvinced. Here again, Pinterest came in handy when Jeni pulled images of spaces that incorporated the plank siding but still aligned with the kids' visions. Similarly, Jeni combined Caysen's fascination with the life and times of Abraham Lincoln with her own love of antique oil portraits and ephemera. An oil painting of old Abe himself hangs on Caysen's wall, opposite a vintage street marker that reads "Lincoln Street." Compromise and conversation enabled the kids to feel respected in their interests, Jeni to feel satisfied in her aesthetics, and everyone to feel happy in the end.

A Practical Demonstration

Jeni handed the reins to her kids in matters of palette, pattern, and peripherals. However, she didn't relinquish complete control, and when they presented her with ideas that defied the realm of possibility, she put on her design-expert hat and pulled out her measuring tape. No matter how outlandish the suggestion, Jeni and Joel treated it as seriously as any other and performed a physical test of its feasibility. Bailey's indoor hammock fell victim to the realities of dormered ceilings. So too did Caysen's dream of a hanging platform bed after a plywood facsimile that Jeni and Joel erected failed to perform. However, Caysen has since picked up on his mother's tricks. Much to Jeni's bemused chagrin, he has provided measurements and to-scale drawings in support of a window seat concept she'd nixed. Caught in a clever web of her own spinning, Jeni relented—and construction on the seat is now pending.

Grow Together: How to Bring It Home

- Include kids in the design process from the outset. Exposing them to resources such as Pinterest, books and magazines, and even store displays enriches their research and creative abilities for school-work and beyond.

- Finding ways to merge your tastes and interests with theirs—artwork and DIYs you create together, curios that reflect

passions you share—will result in a space in which you both feel at home.

- As much as possible, let kids learn decor lessons through trial and error. Giving their ideas credence even though you know they may not work in the end not only builds their confidence, it gives you both the opportunity to strengthen problem-solving skills.

CELEBRA

TE The
Small Space

Everyone has a small-space story to share. Maybe it was that year in college when the housing administration crammed four bunks into dorm rooms built for two. Or perhaps it was that first solo apartment, the one where the landlord charged extra for the closet because technically it could fit a mattress. Or it could be where you're sitting now, in a sixth-floor walkup that tries your patience and tests your resolve with its windowless rooms and airless atmosphere. We keep our memories of these spaces in our back pockets and pull them out at parties, one-upping each other with our tales of toilets in the shower, camp stoves on the counter, roommates at each other's throats.

Indeed whatever the reasons for living small—the location or the low rent, by necessity or by choice—a dearth of elbow room can create a serious challenge. Yet like anything that requires extra effort, small interiors bring with them extra rewards. A studio apartment asks us to think outside the box for seating, storage, and sleep solutions, and it rewards us with the thrill of creativity and confidence that accompanies an ingenious workaround. Living short on space allows us to focus on longer-term aspirations, such as saving for a honeymoon or a house, reducing our environmental footprint, or getting a new business off the ground. And whether it's a transitional consideration or a permanent preference, a tight interior demands that we think long and hard about the difference between want and need. We may start to appreciate how little we actually require to feel safe, secure, and happy.

Fortunately, limited square footage needn't translate into limited style. In fact, the increased thought that goes into decorating a small space often results in a more curated, considered aesthetic. There's no room for "meh" in a minuscule home. When every inch counts, every object is weighed by how well it meets its purpose and aligns with a desired aesthetic. You must learn to keep only what works and only what you truly love—a lesson that can benefit studio and estate dwellers alike.

So take advantage of the gift that a small space brings by stripping away the excess and celebrating what remains. List the ways you plan to use your home and how you can facilitate them—then look for areas of overlap where you can get creative. Can the computer monitor you work on during the day be the television you watch movies on at night? Can your ottoman and living room accent tables double as extra seating? When it comes to storage, where are the hidden opportunities, how can you tap them, and how much can you pare back your belongings according to only what you actually use? Finally, how can you define your desired aesthetic with as few pieces as possible? Approach the design of your small space as a poet does the composition of a haiku, and remember that the strongest statement sometimes springs from the smallest number of words.

This chapter highlights four small-space inhabitants who have eked equal measures of form and function from every corner of their abodes. They include a New Yorker who traded her tiny apartment for an even smaller one so she could indulge her love of travel; a prop stylist who left the family farm for the big city with the goal of taking her career to the next level; a photographer who channeled a laissez-faire mindset in her airy Portland abode; and an art director who relocated from Brooklyn to Seattle but retained the less-is-more mindset of the concrete jungle. Each buried old conceptions and unearthed new values in the process of designing a home that met her needs, and each can attest to the awareness and appreciation that comes with living large when you're living small.

Celebrate Adventure

Pied-à-Terre Perfection

Brooke Fitts is no stranger to minimalist conditions. The wedding and editorial photographer spends a significant portion of each year on the road, crashing with friends and subsisting from her suitcase. Her work and her wanderlust alike have carried her as far afield as Tulum and Oahu, Istanbul and Iceland. As for the five years that she's lived in New York, her rentals have grown progressively smaller as she's watched the city's real estate market evolve from pretty darn crowded to positively cutthroat. Yet Brooke's latest flat demands more of her flexibility than ever before; at four hundred square feet, it makes her previous apartments seem nearly palatial.

However, Brooke has embraced her diminishing environs happily; she actually jumped on this unit the moment she learned of its availability. Though the lofted studio offers less room, its central location in the neighborhood of Brooklyn Heights enables Brooke to rent it to the legions of tourists who flock to the city each year in search of an authentic Big Apple experience. This additional income in turn allows Brooke to pursue her goal of diversifying her travel photography portfolio—and also to live half of each month in Seattle, where Brooke's young daughter resides with her father. With her neutral yet striking decor, she's composed a personal novella within the saga of New York, thereby setting the scene for a one-of-a-kind experience no matter whose head rests on her pillow.

Broad Appeal

Because Brooke opens her apartment to wayfarers from around the globe, she strove for an overall aesthetic that would please but not polarize. She selected earthy shades and tactile materials to satisfy a range of diverse tastes and also to create a warm, welcoming vibe. A coffee table and desk of reclaimed wood sit atop a woven dhurrie in buttery yellow. The rug's fringe echoes that on the ecru throw that Brooke keeps at the ready to toss on her slate-colored wool sofa, while pillows in the same creamy tones further soften the space. Color and texture unite to create a space that speaks the universal language of cozy.

Individual Impression

During her extensive travels, the accommodations that Brooke has enjoyed most have been the ones imbued with the identities of their owners. With that in mind, she's accented the apartment with deeply personal pieces that leave her visitors with a vivid picture of their host (and that help her feel at home when she stays there). The deer hide that drapes the sofa belongs to a species of animal found only in Hawaii, where Brooke was raised. A collection of antique cameras nods to Brooke's career. And all the art originated either from Brooke's lens or from her creative colleagues' paintbrushes and pens. Even a cursory glance at the space reads like a memoir of its occupant's creative and adventuresome life.

Color and texture unite to create a space that speaks the universal language of cozy.

Time Traveler

Much of the apartment's draw stems from its location among the cobbled streets and river walks that comprise Brooklyn's oldest neighborhood. To reinforce this spirit of place for her renters—and to celebrate the city that she herself names as her favorite in the world—Brooke has endeavored to bring a sense of geography and heritage inside the apartment as well. The 1865 structure has lent itself well to a variety of nineteenth-century industrial accents. A weighty iron pharmacy cabinet displays Brooke's cameras rather than the tinctures and ointments it once held. Other galvanized metals punctuate the room, including an aluminum trash can and tin photo boxes. Finally, towers of vintage wood crates and cartons provide additional storage while evoking the markets and milkmen of a bygone era. For anyone seeking an experience of old New York, Brooke's home frames a concise snapshot in modern-day style.

Celebrate Adventure: How to Bring It Home

◆ Whether you open your home to frequent guests or not, approach your design as though you do; there's no reason why you yourself shouldn't enjoy the same welcoming, inviting touches that you'd install for others!

◆ Take a look around your space and envision it through a visitor's eyes. What does it say about your personal values and interests? In a small space every object counts, so only keep the ones that speak most clearly to your passions and beliefs.

◆ No home is an island. Craft a stronger sense of place by bringing in elements of the geography and history of your town. These can be as subtle as a vase from a local ceramicist or as striking as a framed array of historical photographs.

Celebrate Ambition

Relaunch Pad

It's sometimes logistically necessary—and nowadays increasingly common—for adult children to move in with their parents. But as Meagan Camp can attest, it isn't always easy. Meagan rejoined the nest at the age of twenty-seven when she moved from Sacramento back to her childhood home in the Hudson Valley. While the time with her family gave her a chance to regain her footing, it also awakened in her the realization that she'd never determined a true sense of direction. An experienced interiors stylist, Meagan had pursued assignments in California but had found limited offerings. And though she'd dabbled in antiques and retail upon her return to Upstate New York, her heart remained firmly in the world of styling. Meagan knew that to achieve the satisfaction she sought, she needed to go where the opportunity lay: New York City.

Meagan also knew that she wanted to live alone for the first time in her life, no matter how prohibitive her budget as a single freelancer. The desire to focus on her career without the interference of family, a roommate, or a live-in romantic partner left her more than willing to trade elbow room for independence. She secured a three-hundred-square-foot apartment on Manhattan's Upper East Side, one that decades of renovations had rendered void of personality. But with a thoughtful decorating scheme and a few tricks of her trade, the stylist fashioned a space that anchors her ambitions with a sense of calm focus. And as she put the finishing touches on her home, she signaled the end of her transition and the start of an exciting new chapter.

Setting Boundaries

Because every successful room begins with a carefully devised furniture arrangement, Meagan established three distinct areas for sitting, working, and sleeping. However, in a studio as small as this one, a strategic floor plan isn't enough. So Meagan carved out the space vertically as well. She first applied a coat of soft gray paint to a segment of wall behind the sofa. The shade doesn't contrast markedly with the white of the remaining walls; rather, it differs only enough to set the living area apart from the rest of the apartment. A shelf over the couch mirrors an identical one mounted above the desk, both of them serving to delineate their respective functional zones while still maintaining a sense of symmetry between the seating area and the workspace. Finally, a pair of swing-arm sconces flank the bed. Meagan chose to not hardwire the lamps and instead left the cords exposed for their framing effect. By thinking upward as well as outward, Meagan simulated the depth and dimension of a much larger interior.

Shore It Up

With nothing but long, arduous workdays in her foreseeable future, Meagan wanted her home to provide a relaxing counterpoint to the rigors of life on set. She therefore called upon her fondness for the beach and its sweeping vistas to inspire design elements that set a tranquil mood—and that conveniently lend an open, airy quality to the small flat. Enter the apartment and soak in a soothing palette of neutrals such as surf, sky, and shell. Underfoot, a sisal area rug brings to mind the fibrous reeds of sea grass and the coarse grit of sand between the toes. Sheer, gauzy curtains billow like sails in the breeze from the open windows, and a pair of alabaster desk lamps mimic the wave-worn finish of stones. Without a single literal reference to the ocean, Meagan has summoned the expansive and restorative nature of a place where the eye can rest and the mind can wander.

By thinking upward as well as outward, Meagan simulated the depth and dimension of a much larger interior.

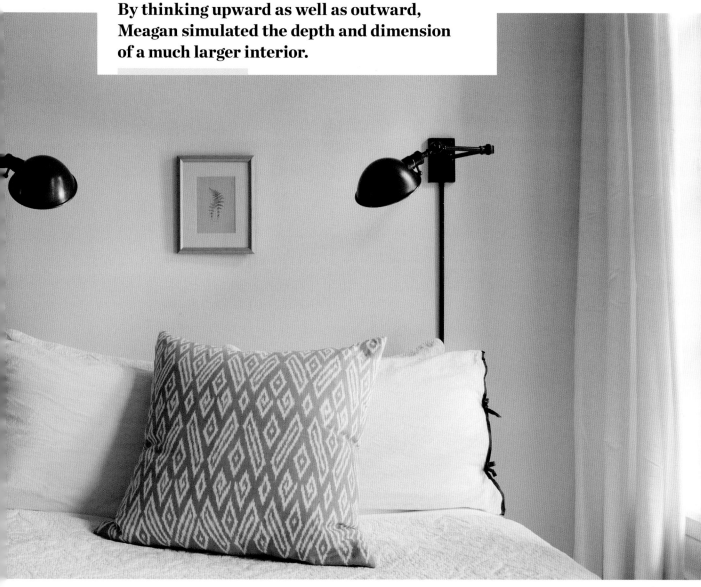

Period of Reflection

Small-space dwellers and interiors experts alike have long relied on the ability of mirrors to create the illusion of additional space. Meagan took this time-honored technique to the next level by not merely incorporating reflective surfaces into her decor but also giving ample consideration to their size, style, and positioning. A mirror six feet in height rests perpendicular to the sofa, its unframed construction making it less a decor feature and more a seamless component of the room's perimeter. Meagan chose to lean rather than mount the mirror, thereby bouncing the sunlight from the opposing windows onto the ceiling and back down to the seating area below. The simple yet clever maneuver both enlarges and illuminates the portion of the apartment in which Meagan spends most of her at-home waking hours. By contrast, a small antique mirror hangs next to the bed, where its petite proportions emulate the intimate mood appropriate to a bedroom, and its vintage patina casts a diffuse glow conducive to peaceful slumber. In the absence of walls to define her space, Meagan found that a sheet or two of glass does just fine.

Celebrate Ambition: How to Bring It Home

◆ A small space can still make a strong stylistic statement; each piece just needs to work a little harder. Have a clear picture of the look you'd like to create, and only bring home items that further that aesthetic goal.

◆ Manipulate the quality of light in different corners of your space to carve out separate functional zones. Bright and ample illumination in the living and work areas strikes an energetic daytime note, while a single glowing sconce near the bed sets a relaxed tone.

◆ Mirrors truly can make a room seem twice as large as it actually is. If you'd rather not catch constant glances at yourself, mix a few small mirrors in with a gallery wall of artwork, placing them closer to the ceiling, where they'll still bounce light around the room.

Celebrate
Afresh

Goodbye, Hello

The route from Nashville to Portland makes for a long drive, especially in November—and especially when everything familiar recedes into the distance with each passing mile. Laura Dart took this very trip to close the gap in a cross-country relationship, leaving behind an established photography career as well as a large, full house, and arriving in Oregon with only her camera and a few essentials. Laura spent the next while accumulating a new client base and new belongings, and slowly her homesickness for Nashville softened.

When her romantic relationship ended, Laura chose to remain in the Pacific Northwest not only for the creative community into which she'd entrenched herself but also for the majestic natural beauty that had firmly implanted itself in her heart. However, the decision meant downsizing yet again, this time to a tiny apartment located in a turn-of-the-century boardinghouse. The two years since have been a study in compromise as she's squeezed an office and photo studio from the single room where she also eats and sleeps; sorted through her extraneous accessories and the emotions that accompany them; and learned exactly what she needs to make Portland feel like home.

The apartment illustrates that carefully chosen large pieces needn't dwarf a tight interior.

Work with It

Instead of trying to put her mark on the space with copious extras, Laura has made the most of her small flat by finding ways to venerate its existing features. Although the kitchen's narrow floor plan prohibits much cooking, Laura adores it for its quirky personality and has augmented it with hardware and hangings that enhance its existing character. Similarly, the floors in the kitchen and bathroom appeal to Laura's fondness for unusual tile work, so she's carried their charm into the living room with a rug that boasts an identical pattern. Finally, Laura's favorite feature in the apartment—the fireplace—has received the royal treatment. This inherent focal point becomes all the more prominent with an array of artwork and favorite objects adorning its mantel and hearth. Evenings find Laura watching the flames in lieu of a TV, and appreciating what her space does offer rather than what it doesn't.

Living Large

Many studio dwellers scale down their furniture to suit their surroundings, but Laura wasn't willing to sacrifice the homey comfort she draws from oversized pieces. She's successfully incorporated a few unexpectedly bulky elements into her home, and the apartment illustrates that carefully chosen large pieces needn't dwarf a tight interior. A long farm table easily seats eight yet feels inconspicuous among a monochromatic mix of chairs and an otherwise bare dining area. A hefty raw-edge coffee table squats before the fireplace but enjoys plenty of clearance with only a single round chair and cleanly upholstered sofa encircling it. With a careful edit Laura has made the flat her own, and in the process has proven that a small space doesn't require small furnishings to feel big.

Forest for the Trees

One of Laura's favorite aspects of her space isn't located in the apartment at all but rather just beyond it: the canopy of ancient trees that catches the afternoon breeze and filters sunlight through her third-floor windows. She picked up this environmental cue and ran with it, using almost exclusively warm pine decor to merge her interior with the exterior. First, the coffee and dining tables set the tone; then, midsized elements including a kitchen cart, floor lamp, and apple-crate bookshelves align with the theme. Small accents get in on the act too, with photo frames, plant stands, and even slices of fallen logs from the Pacific Northwest rainforest completing the picture. In the shelter of her treehouse home, Laura doesn't just bring the outdoors in, she effectively makes the walls disappear.

Celebrate Afresh: How to Bring It Home

- Emphasize the features you do like about your space rather than lament the ones you don't. Keep that charming vintage medicine cabinet extra tidy and you're less likely to dwell on the dimly lit shower. Think of it as a gratitude practice for your home!

- Oversized pieces *can* feel at home in a small space, but allow them to speak for themselves and keep the surrounding decor especially simple—be it with a sparse color palette or minimalist accents.

- Make the most of the openings in your home's exterior envelope to invoke a sense of seamlessness with the outdoors. Keep curtains or blinds simple if you use them at all, and include organic touches that relate to the view beyond your windows.

Celebrate Again

Back to the Future

Being the new kid is never easy. Being the new kid in your old hometown brings an entirely separate set of challenges, one with which Jordan Carlson became acquainted when she returned to Seattle after a four-year hiatus in Brooklyn. The art director initially headed east to attend design school, as well as to seek a change of pace and a change of scene. She made friends and found work easily, but she never quite settled into an urban rhythm or stopped craving the open skies of her former town. So Jordan packed up once again and beat a path back west.

She landed in a city that looked much as she'd left it and yet very different too. Old friends had traded midnight bar crawls for midnight breast feedings, and within her once-childless network, Jordan now found herself the carefree single auntie. However, Jordan had changed as well; her years in New York's narrow urban corridor had by necessity winnowed her life into a more compact, cohesive existence. In designing her recently acquired apartment in Seattle's Capitol Hill, Jordan applied both the curiosity that first carried her to Brooklyn as well as the crystallized vision she acquired there. The intimate, eclectic flat reveals a sense of space and sense of self that are at once clearly defined and wholly open to possibility.

The flat reveals a sense of space and sense of self that are at once clearly defined and wholly open to possibility.

Saving Space

During her sojourn in Brooklyn, Jordan became a master at maximizing the possibilities of awkward areas. While her new home does deliver a little more leeway, she's viewed it with the same solutions-oriented eye that she honed previously. An industrial flat file serves as a coffee table as well as storage; Jordan added wheels to the cabinet so she can easily move it aside should she require more open floor. She also has a second castered unit on which she keeps her TV, though this one she relegates to a closet so as to hide the unattractive appliance when it's not in use. Finally, a utilitarian dual-shelved nightstand functions as both an end table and a bookcase in the living room. Even with more space at her fingertips, Jordan still derives style and satisfaction from practical, multipurpose pieces.

Shade and Shadow

As a graphic designer Jordan knows the power of color to soothe even as it excites. Never one to take the neutral route, she also recognized that her apartment needed a cohesive theme to unify the small rooms. A palette of somber grays and pensive blues therefore dominates, creating flow while still adding intrigue. The combination of a steely sofa and a misty rug shores up the living room. Meanwhile, in the bedroom, gleaming charcoal walls provide a dramatic backdrop for textured linens in slate and granite. The color scheme encourages the eye to travel smoothly from one hue to the next for an expansive effect, but at the same time engages with its subtle sense of drama.

Hospitality On Call

Jordan has always counted herself as the primary connector in her social group and as such loves to play hostess. With her own tight interior and her friends' time demands rendering large formal gatherings difficult, she's become adept at welcoming visitors no matter their number or the length of their stay. In the living area she has prioritized multiple seating options over other furnishings and accessories. Three chairs and two ottomans circle the sofa for endless conversation configurations, while slim-legged accent tables and hairpin lighting prevent the area from feeling packed— and leave leeway for additional seating to be brought in from the bedroom. Jordan has also equipped the kitchen so that guests can appreciate her personal touch in small but significant ways, including a collection of one-of-a-kind coffee cups that lets each visitor stake a claim to her own individual mug every time she stops by. Jordan has established a home that facilitates quality interactions on a whim, no matter the space and scheduling limitations she encounters.

Celebrate Again: How to Bring It Home

- The question of whether to have a TV comes up often in a small space. A mobile media stand lets you have your cake and watch it too! If you can't find a wheeled cart that suits your style, remember that casters can be purchased separately and installed relatively easily.

- A tight, cohesive color palette gives a small space a composed quality, and it needn't be a neutral one. Mix colors that share the same level of saturation—all jewel tones or exclusively pastels, for example—for a dynamic look that still feels intentional.

- A fluid furniture arrangement that includes stackable stools, accent tables that double as seating, and slim silhouettes throughout gives small-space dwellers the opportunity to entertain multiple guests at a time.

Resources

The homeowners featured in this book have named the following retailers among their favorite sources for everything from affordable basics to one-of-a-kind finds.

Amelia
Find art prints, unique office supplies, and handmade ephemera at the online outpost of this charming Oxford, Mississippi shop. Boutique owner Erin Abbott Kirkpatrick's home appears on pages 160–165.
ameliapresents.com

Anthropologie
Treasures for creating memorable tabletops and vignettes abound at Anthropologie. Shop the sale section for bargains on hardware, knick-knacks, and coffee table books.
anthropologie.com

Blu Dot
This Minnesota-based company produces modern furnishings that won't break the bank for a Scandinavian-meets-American vibe.
www.bludot.com

Brika
Founded by a two female entrepreneurs from Canada, Brika impeccably curates a playful yet sophisticated selection of artwork, textiles, and ceramics—all of it from independent artisans.
brika.com

Chairish
Score everything from mod sofas to midcentury lighting at a resale home goods site, then use the Chairish app to offload your own items when you're ready for a fresh look.
www.chairish.com

Crate & Barrel
A go-to for solidly and sustainably constructed furnishings such as bed frames and case goods, as well as thoughtful decor for entertaining and seasonal updates.
www.crateandbarrel.com

Elsie Green
French table linens mingle with Victorian flatware at this Bay Area vintage boutique, which combines a sustainability ethos with Continental élan.
www.elsiegreen.com

Ethanollie
If a bohemian artist and a Pacific Northwest woodsman got married, they'd furnish their love nest with vintage plant hangers and camp blankets from this Portland Etsy seller.
www.etsy.com/shop/ethanollie

The Foundry Home Goods
Utilitarian simplicity meets functional elegance at this Minneapolis-based boutique, where you'll find everything from fragrant beeswax candles to handmade cutting boards.
www.thefoundryhomegoods.com

Heath Ceramics
Minimalist refinement marks plates, glasses, and servingware from a San Francisco company favored by chefs as well as diners since the 1940s.
www.heathceramics.com

IKEA
A seemingly endless supply of affordable, design-savvy staples from curtains to storage containers—and a surprisingly complete resource for full-scale kitchen renovations.
www.ikea.com

Lamps Plus
Don't let the name fool you. In addition to offering lighting for every room of the house, this family-owned and operated site also sells furniture, artwork, mirrors, and more.
www.lampsplus.com

Love the Design
Shop estate sale, farmhouse, and factory finds to foster the industrial-luxe vibe that characterizes founder Christine Flynn's bedroom on pages 126–131.
www.lovethedesign.com

Lulu & Georgia
A youthful, feminine sensibility pervades this online decor mainstay, which boasts an especially large selection of rugs and throw pillows.
www.luluandgeorgia.com

Maven Collection
Add global intrigue with Maven's colorful collection of Moroccan poufs, rugs, and textiles. Proceeds benefit indigenous artisans and their communities.
mavencollection.com

Oh, Albatross
A sense of stylish serenity defines the vintage and handmade toys, art, and small decor items from this Michigan-based Etsy seller.
www.etsy.com/shop/ohalbatross

One Kings Lane
Design industry experts put their personal collections up for grabs, and clearance prices on international interiors brands can't be beat.
www.onekingslane.com

Restoration Hardware
Stock up on thirsty Turkish towels—or splurge on sumptuous Belgian bed linens—from this home store known for its historically inspired design.
www.restorationhardware.com

Rugs Direct
Floor coverings of every style and size imaginable comprise the vast inventory of this online retailer; navigate it with the site's exhaustive yet extremely user-friendly search function.
www.rugs-direct.com

Schoolhouse Electric & Supply Co.
Exactly as its name suggests, Schoolhouse Electric is a one-stop shop for light fixtures, clocks, and other home essentials with midcentury form-meets-function appeal.
www.schoolhouseelectric.com

Scoutmob Shoppe
Scoutmob's nationwide curatorial team sorts through countless submissions to deliver locally produced and style-minded goods ranging from bookshelves to duvet covers.
http://scoutmob.com

Serena & Lily
Artistic touches accent luxury bedding for the whole family, while a global undercurrent marks heirloom-worthy entertaining and decorating pieces.
www.serenaandlily.com

Sherwin-Williams Paints
Receive personalized in-store attention on more than 1,500 paint shades from an American company that has specialized in finishes since 1866.
www.sherwin-williams.com

Taylor + Taylor
Inject unique personality with this site's rotating selection of vintage homewares, all with an antiquarian edge. See the home of founders Jessica and Jonathan Taylor on pages 48–53.
www.taylorandtaylor.co

West Elm
A mix of enduring style and on-trend accents—as well as coveted designer collaborations—make West Elm a favorite of professional and amateur decorators alike.
www.westelm.com

Acknowledgments

This book would not exist without the small army of troopers who marched the long and arduous road with me—and who bolstered me throughout the many obstacles. They include my agent Kimberly Perel of Wendy Sherman Associates, who lent her ceaseless support and encouragement. Emily Johnston and Alan Jensen, who saw my vision and brought it to life with their photographic talents. Laura Lee Mattingly, Sara Golski, Allison Weiner, and the rest of the Chronicle team, who carried this book to the world. The friends and colleagues, new and old, who generously opened their homes and their hearts so that I might tell their stories. My mother and father, who armed me with the courage and creativity that a project like this requires. And Ivan, who believed in me from the beginning and who stood by me long after I'd given up on myself. I am forever indebted to them all.